Headwaters Fall as Snow

By

Kathy Scott

Illustrations by Kim Mellema

Alder Creek Publishing

Printed in the United States of America

Illustrations and jacket design by Kim Mellema
Typesetting and technical design by Dan Terpstra
Author's photograph by David Van Burgel
Proofreading by Johannah Oster

10 9 8 7 6 5 4 3 2 1

Library of Congress Cataloging-in Publication Data

Scott, Kathy J., 1954-
    Headwaters Fall as Snow / Kathy Scott

    ISBN (Hard Cover) 0-9657663-3-0

    © 2003
    1. Outdoor Life 2. Natural History 3. Nature Writing
    4. Fly Fishing

I. Title
818

                                            LCCN: 2003103134
                                                       CIP

Also by Kathy Scott,
    Moose in the Water/Bamboo on the Bench
    A Journal and a Journey

Prologue: The Last Days of Summer

Early Winter

Mid Winter

Late Winter

Epilogue: The First Days of Summer

*If you're searching
for the headwaters,
you haven't far to go.*

*Everywhere in the North,
headwaters fall as snow.*

FOREWARD

The significance of any literary work can be measured by its emotional appeal. Even the most didactic of works appeal to some readers, but the more universal the appeal the greater the book.

Kathy Scott in her first book, *Moose in the Water/Bamboo on the Bench* demonstrates a sensitivity that captivates the reader, and *Headwaters Fall as Snow* only reinforces her deep abiding love for nature and for life. The book is built around the poem:

> *If you're searching for the headwaters*
> *You haven't far to go*
> *Everywhere, in the North,*
> *Headwaters fall as snow.*

Beginning with a delightful fishing trip in the late months of summer, the story takes us through the long nights of winter until again come the soft zephyrs of spring. Ms Scott with her deft touch weaves her tale on various levels, each of which has its own charm and appeal. Kathy's story is basically a story of love, the love of a man and woman, the love of family, the love of a dog and his master, the love of all things God has created and the mastering and upholding of an arcane craft. The melding of all these themes is as masterful as a puppeteer's management of his marionette strings. We come to know the deep and abiding love of Kat and David for each other; to appreciate the complete union of their lives. We come to know of their family and their friends and we can vicariously share in the influence that they have on Kat and David's lives. We rejoice with their dog Kodiak's zest for chasing mink through chest deep snow. Our senses respond to the sights, sounds, smells and emotions that Kat evokes as she makes her daily trips around Big Pond. And finally we empathize with David's devotion to his craft knowing full well the tribulation that exists in the search for perfection.

The real charm of *Headwaters Fall as Snow* is Kathy's ability to weave all of these various themes together to invoke in the reader a poignant, emotional response. The reader comes to empathize with all that Kathy writes of. We feel the bite of the winter cold, and thrill to the sights and sounds of chickadees as they gather around the feeder and alight on Kat's hand. The smoke of the wood burning stove recalls (at least to the older of us) the times with family at Grandmother's house. David splitting cane and Kat working at her old school desk in the empty, but warm, North House affirms that love need not be passion. *Headwaters Fall as Snow* makes a perfect companion for *Moose on the Water/Bamboo on the Bench* and both volumes, and David and Kat, too, have enriched my life, for which I am grateful.

— Ralph W. Moon
   Curator, Federation of Fly Fishers Museum, retired

ACKNOWLEDGEMENTS

In my writing, I have had a heartfelt desire to share my awe and passion for the natural world and the simple truths, which make life real. Embrace the wild. Cherish the fragile places, along with close friends and family, so precious yet so inclined to slip away if left unnoticed. In celebrating the most challenging and revealing of seasons, these kindred spirits have assured that I am never alone in facing the greater difficulty of transforming my beliefs into words. My thanks to:

David VanBurgel, without whom there would be no story.

Ron Barch, publisher and Kim Mellema, our treasured artist.

Tom Helgeson and Jerry Kustrich, for sage annotations and support.

Nick Lyons, Ralph Moon and Jerry Dennis for their kind words.

Jennifer Haney and Chris Hutchins, for encouragement from the start and nearly every day afterwards. Also, Norma Stankevitz, Pamela Witham, David Johnston, Susan Morris, Dean Baker, and the students and staff of Lawrence Junior High School, for their precious gift of time.

Gene Lagomarsino, for invaluable help and telephone breaks.

Burton and Susan Scott, Marilyn and Archie McLachlan, Dorothy VanBurgel, Janet Olsen and Alden Rohen, all willing contributors to early drafts.

And, of course, the ever-patient makers of split bamboo fly rods devoted artisans of the natural world.

Kathy Scott

The Last Days of Summer

There's just something about honestly

encountering conditions as they are,

not beating them, but slipping in neatly

and feeling more or less at home.

— John Gierach

The Willow Maze

"We crossed the sedge meadow to the next thicket where the willows grew taller and the trail more braided."

W e'd thought about fishing Wyoming's Tongue River for a couple of years, ever since we chanced to pull off the highway and check it out on a rapid run toward Yellowstone. A larger than usual cutthroat had made a brief appearance, sliding out from under the overhanging bank on the opposite shore just long enough to imprint itself on our fishing subconscious and haunt us ever since. The clincher, though, was the lady at the National Forest information desk.

"The Tongue?" she answered, "there are lots of big fish over there. Lots." She gestured as if the creek was overflowing with cutts to the point where they could be taken for granted.

We stopped at the access to open the heavy green metal cattlegate. I pulled it clear while David drove the truck through. Kodiak was on his feet in the back of the truck, whining with uncontrollable dog-enthusiasm. He's a lot more honest than we are about expressing excitement. After swinging the gate shut again, I ran the chain around the double wooden post and secured it before jumping back in with David.

We drove on down the two-track to a perch above the river, where two other vehicles were already parked, and assessed the situation. The Tongue was somewhere ahead, hidden behind a seemingly impenetrable wall of willows which stretched out of sight in either direction, upstream and down. Beyond the willows, sage covered hills rose high into mountains, so far away that the cattle grazing here and there on the long slopes looked tiny and would hold no interest for a curious canine.

The occupants of the other trucks were nowhere in sight, so we hopped out and went around back to let Kodiak do the same. David had flipped the cap window up and barely lowered the tailgate when Kodes shot out and began systematically tackling the task of marking every sagebrush as his own.

The willows weren't actually an impenetrable wall, as they had seemed, but a maze of angler and game trails. We decided on a reconnaissance run, sans gear, just in case the river wasn't worth the scramble. Kodiak led the way, disappearing and reappearing through the dense willows, until we all emerged on wet sedges between the thickets.

We crossed the sedge meadow to the next thicket where the willows grew taller and the trail was more braided. We maneuvered our way through single file, David just keeping Kodiak in sight and me doing the same with David. We stooped and zigzagged. I was glad we didn't have rigged rods with the willows towering over my head and their clumps spread so wide and low that I had to duck down between and under the branches.

We emerged once again, miraculously together although somewhat irritated this time, near riffles between two pools so full of big trout that we immediately forgot the approach.

"Look at that. Look at that," David pointed.

I was properly beside myself, and we turned to make a fast as possible run back to the truck for our gear. Kodiak led with equal enthusiasm, so I was surprised when he disappeared through a narrow passage in the willows and then re-appeared running toward me. Then I saw the cow moose in hot pursuit. I stopped short, and Kodiak ran behind me.

"Moose!" I yelled, as much to alert David, somewhere following me, as to address the cow, which may not have been aware that there was a human ahead. She wasn't, and stopped. Kodiak attempted to trot back toward her just as David yelled back that there was a moose calf standing on the riverbank. The river and David seemed very far away. The crowned willows muffled his voice, and I couldn't see him or hear the water.

"We're getting out of here," I yelled, hoping he could hear. In the back of my mind I rationalized. At least, if sound wasn't getting through, no other anglers would have to be listening to this. I nabbed Kodiak by the collar and ducked under the brush, heading roughly in the direction of the truck. Kodiak wanted to lead, his genetic predisposition, so I let him go, reasoning that the moose would stay with her calf. The moment I stopped for breath, I could still hear her coming. I told Kodiak to keep low and run, and I did the same.

We emerged on to the sedges just before David.

"I couldn't make you hear me," he said. "I hope you didn't think I was the moose."

Call it flexibility under fire, like caribou returning to their grazing after one of their number has been taken by wolves, or just call it fish fever. The entire incident was immediately brushed aside as we dove into the smaller set of willows determined to gear up and return to the cutts, four legged obstacles notwithstanding.

The plan was made as we pulled on our waders and boots. I would leash Kodiak; David would carry the rods. We'd scout the river and trade off dog-care if the moose were still there or the anglers were close. I chose the Payne 97 bamboo rod David had made me a few years ago, and he decided on a 7-foot 3-weight cane rod made by Al Medved, nice for tight quarters. I weeded through my vest pockets for extraneous gear and decided to jettison a few fly boxes before dropping off the sagebrush and back into the willows.

David was rigged before Kodiak and I were untangled from the maze. There were no moose or anglers at the Tongue, and the pools were so clear that the trout resting just above the bottom were vivid in every detail. They were aloof and beautiful, ignoring the admiring world above. They seemed oblivious to Kodiak's presence, as most fish are, when he plunged into the pool with them and paddled around. Good. They weren't shy. I've been known to use Kodiak for cover.

David headed upstream, where one lone cutt was feeding on the surface. He cast a dry fly perfectly into its feeding lane. It was ignored. He tried a few more casts while I tied on a tiny white emerger.

"Nothing works," he called down to me. "Look at all of these fish. This big one won't take anything I drift over it."

I waded up to the shallow gravel near his pool. There were six fish there, big fish, fourteen-inch fish in a ten-foot wide stream. One was periodically rising to something neither of us could see on the surface.

"Go ahead and try him," David offered. "I'm going to tie on a new tippet."

He went up on the bank, and I took his spot. The fish rose, I cast, and the fly floated by. The fish rose, I re-cast, and the fly floated by. David came back into the water and offered to head farther upstream if I was still working the pool. I wasn't really; I was just getting in a little casting practice with a stubborn fish target, but I wasn't tired of it yet, so he passed by.

The second my witness was gone, my timing and the fish's timing reached one of those rare, unexpected junctures. Either I cast the fly and he took it, or he came up to take something else and my fly floated into his mouth. Suddenly he was on, and I could tell he was a real fish. The water boiled. David and Kodiak had time to come watch. It had been a while since I'd hooked such a powerful fish, and never before on cane.

Then we were fumbling getting the camera off my neck and over my hat and setting David's rod where Kodiak couldn't run over it in the close quarters of the willows, and trying to release the cutt, pose for the photo (no, Kodiak, you can't have the fish), and find the hemostats (this must be a store fly; it still has a barb), and it was gone.

A real fish, a fifteen-inch cutthroat on a dry fly. Cool.

As it turned out, it was the only fish in the Tongue which wasn't too aloof to associate with us. The rest, dozens of them, didn't even bother to turn up their noses. They ignored us. We decided to break for lunch, and we were back in the willows again.

At the truck, we dropped the waders and vests, and lounged on the tailgate. Kodiak climbed into the back and collapsed on the bed to sleep it off. We heard voices coming from the willows, and the occupants of the other vehicles finally materialized. They had seen us on the creek and had leap-frogged past us during the photoshoot. We had no idea; we never heard them or saw them.

"There was a big bull moose right by you, too," one of them said, "but you were going the other way or we'd have told you. Had a nice rack." Those willows could hide anything.

We stalled for a while, licking our willow wounds, but it was a hard thing to resolve. A freestone stream, big cutthroats, and only one strike all day. Finally, we headed back, thinking maybe evening would be different.

We'd just made it through the sedges, apparently not on the same trails as before, when we came across Bull Creek. It was a third of the Tongue's size, but the other anglers told us that it was rumored to be worth trying, although they hadn't themselves.

Mistake #1: I decided to wade down the Bull and test my luck. It was tiny, and I didn't have a fairy rod, but why not? David offered to give Kodiak a free run and meet me at the Tongue to swap turns. I stored the leash around my waist, then tied on a little parachute caddis. I decided in the first two minutes that things were not good. My line tangled in the willows overhanging the quick twists and turns of the creek, my rod caught repeatedly on the branches, and, in just those two or three minutes, David was completely gone.

"David," I called out. I needed to tell him I was bailing. No reply. I struggled to collect my line and rod and stepped out of the water into the clumps of willows where I'd last seen David. Which way did he go? I'd been so intent on negotiating the tight quarters of the creek that I really had no clue. Downstream, to be sure, somehow.

I couldn't hold my rod up over the brush, so I guided it by the reel and ducked under, trailing the tip behind. I had just started following roughly downstream when I stumbled on to a mat of packed grass. Moose bed. Freshly used. I'm not afraid of moose, just highly respectful of them. We see them all of the time in the pond at home, and I've never once been chased. I've never jumped one with a calf in a willow thicket before either.

"David!" I tried. I really wanted to tell him I was choosing a new route. I whistled for Kodiak. Nothing. I continued downstream. Unfortunately, I had just freed myself from some intertwined willow arms when I stepped into some steaming, calf-sized moose droppings. Okay, time to detour. I abandoned the moose trail, fought the brush perpendicular to the river until I completed a sufficient detour, and swung back to the Tongue.

No David. No Kodiak. I tried calling out again, but I knew the riffles would take care of any noise the willows let through. There was no seeing around the bends in the Tongue, although I could look over the willows and see the mountaintops as landmarks back to the truck. Still, we'd planned a rendezvous at the Bull, so I headed downstream.

Mistake #2: About half way to the bull, I decided that David would have surely gone upstream toward the catch and release water by now, so I turned back and headed that way. Willow logic. I passed the point where I had found the stream and tried calling again.

"David," I yelled, with little enthusiasm, looking at the cutts lying there, snobs that they were, and wishing I was fishing. I looked up to see a young angler staring downstream at me.

"Lost my husband," I grinned. "And my dog. Seen them?"

He was mercifully polite, but hadn't. He agreed to tell David that I'd gone back to the truck, and, as I turned to go, added, "I did see a cow and calf moose, though."

I took a fix on the peaks I knew were situated directly over the truck and plunged back into the maze of willows toward it. The branches tried to snatch my hat, my sunglasses, and, finally, my fly rod. I'd seen David varnish it five times and knew the willows were no match for the finish, but they stole the fly and tangled the line, so I stopped and broke the rod down. Two pieces would be easier to negotiate than one. The halves pulled apart with a characteristic pop, and I took a step forward into an explosion of screeching birds.

Four fledgling hawks tried frantically to fly somewhere, anywhere, in the confusion of the willow understory with a human suddenly stepping into their brushy sanctuary. Each was dark brown with a striped tail and as large as an adult. One that could have used more time in flight school crashed into my path, tried to fly under the next clump, and ricocheted off the branches right back into my path. Another detour.

There was no sense in traumatizing the teenager further, so I crawled off to the right and tried to circle around through the maze one more time. I emerged on the sedge meadow, a bit worse for wear, but so preoccupied with hawk identification that I chanced on to a decent path right through the second set of willows and up to the truck.

Someone was sitting on a lawn chair in front of a truck parked next to ours. I said hello and couldn't help smiling, wondering what he thought of me as I tossed my rod and vest on to the front seat and caught sight of myself in the mirror. Fairly disheveled. I grabbed a two-way radio, positioned the other where David would find it, left a note, and shut the door.

"Lost my husband." I was still smiling.

"He'll probably find his way back," he said. It seemed reasonable.

"Yeah, he probably will," I agreed. "But he might think I'm still down there, and be waiting with our dog. Lost my dog, too," I paused and glanced down at my waist. "Lost my dog leash, too." I sighed. "Could you tell him there's a note on the truck seat, please, if he comes up here?"

He said he would, and I looked across the willows and sedges to where the Tongue was hiding, a long, long way away. Then I dove back into the maze.

I was downstream at the confluence with the Bull when I heard David's voice over the radio in my pocket.

"You there?" he asked calmly.

There was a Coke in my hand, my waders were hanging next to David's on the pickup's mirror, and Kodiak was reassured and sleeping when the last angler came up from the willows. I knew him, the polite guy.

"Found my husband," I said, "and my dog. Lost my dog leash, though."

True to form, he excused me. "It was probably the only thing the fish ate today," he smiled back.

That night, lying on the bed in the back of the truck at the trailhead, lulled by the sounds of coyotes and a thunderstorm far in the distance, David asked, "What do you think? Where should we fish tomorrow?"

"Let's try it here again," I said, drifting off. "It was fun."

EARLY WINTER

―――――

That's the best thing about walking,

the journey itself.

It doesn't matter whether you get

where you're going or not.

You'll get there anyway.

Every good hike brings you

eventually back home.

Right where you started.

— Edward Abbey

Home Again

"Hilton brook begins in mossy springs and hidden pools beneath the summit of Hampshire Hill."

Nodding ladies' tresses. I found the new flower in both the Peterson and Audubon field guides to wildflowers, and it was unmistakable. The tiny white orchid holding its stubby stalk straight and its heavy head of curly tresses high was new and special. It was a crisp fall evening in Maine, and David was back at the bench planing cane for a new fly rod.

Just one week before, only seven days, we were at the end of a long summer with too much left to do, and all of it wonderful. David was lapping the ferrules on a three piece four-weight, a beautiful, darkly flamed work of art. I had just finished an informal inventory of the world defined by our beaver ponds. It was an affair of the heart, and one that good company and other activities had forced me to postpone, adding to the satisfaction I felt after finally completing my survey.

Home again. Maine. The Hilton Brook begins in the mossy springs and hidden pools beneath the summit of Hampshire Hill, winds into a brook as it enters our chain of beaver ponds, then flows on to the north. It disappears into the Mercer Bog, traveling long, slender miles between two ridges left by glaciers and lined by red-winged blackbirds balancing near the tops of cattails. Farther north, it joins the waters of the Sandy River. The Sandy, in turn, flows into the Kennebec River near the abandoned site of the village of Norridgewock.

The Abenaki, people of the dawn, once lived there. The land was among the most beautiful in Maine, then part of the Colony of Massachusetts, but had the misfortune of lying on the line between two powerful nations with very different perspectives. The French, interested in furs and souls, hoped to maintain their presence in the person of a Jesuit priest, Father Sebastian Rasle. From his mission on the banks of the Kennebec, he gained the respect of the Abenaki, wrote the first dictionary of their language, and supported their resistance to the English.

The English first came to the Maine part of Massachusetts shortly after the Mayflower had arrived in Plimouth, now Plymouth, around 1608. They had already met Squanto, originally from that area, and a second native named Samoset, from the land of the Abenaki. Boats came up the Kennebec River as far as they could penetrate; the English wanted land to settle. The upstream Kennebec Abenaki weren't receptive to their intentions, and their progress was halted.

In 1724, Bomazeem, a chief who had recently returned from negotiations with the English which had evolved into years of imprisonment in a Boston jail, was camped below the mission village with his wife and young daughter when the English lost patience and sent militia upriver. When he realized he couldn't save his family, Bomazeem tried to warn his village, Norridgewock, upriver at Old Point. He didn't make it across the rips which now bear his name, and a monument to Father Rasle stands over the grave where the few returning Abenaki buried the slain priest before leaving to join their kindred elsewhere.

The cross from the Norridgewock Mission resides with the Penobscots, Abenaki on Indian Island in Old Town. That watershed is just to the east and leads up-river to the heart of the forest explored by Henry David Thoreau about a hundred years later. His accounts of his travels to the Maine Woods include native place name translations attributed to Father Rasle. Thoreau met H. L. Leonard, often called the father of the six-sided split bamboo fly rod, and hired canoes out of Old Town; we go to Old Town for canoes, on occasion, still.

History is as much a part of this place as the granite bedrock. From our front decks, we look southwest to Hampshire Hill, rising high above our ponds. Before the Civil War, it was covered in apples, one of the biggest orchards east of the Mississippi. But men like Joshua Chamberlain's boys of the 20th Maine met young men like those from the 4th Michigan at Gettysburg and learned of farmland where you could plow without hitting rocks of granite and actually get mud in your eye, and they moved west. Since the frontier first touched its soil, southern Michigan gained loggers and farmers and place names like Bangor, and Hampshire Hill and much of Maine's other cultivated land returned to forest. By the time we traveled in the reverse direction, Maine was seventy per cent forested again.

And thanks to the blackflies, many of the northern forests had hardly been touched.

We fell in love with Maine on a hiking trip to the majestic peaks of Mount Katahdin. What was good enough for Thoreau was good enough for us. At a point when the bottom fell out of Michigan's automobile industry, we were graduates without job prospects, and Maine needed us. We eventually found some land with great potential, although it needed a little TLC. The loggers had been ruthless, and we picked up discarded plastic bar-oil containers for two years. But the land sloped to the west and south and overlooked a chain of beaver ponds which stretched on for thirty acres.

We fashioned a little clearing and built a snug home. We carried slash, burning great piles each winter, and selectively encouraged the balsam firs and beech, hemlocks, and oaks to grow. Moose laid the first trails around the pond, so we had only to nudge the pathways here and there and keep them trimmed for our long evening walks. An adjacent piece of land, flowing with the sparkling waters of the brook leading into our ponds, became available and became ours. With so much room, we knew we had space to spare and to share, and Kodiak moved from his temporary home at the animal shelter to ours.

Kodiak had only been with us three weeks when we decided to introduce him to the family, and we headed to Michigan for an unexpected visit. Michigan is our other home, the place where we both grew up. We return there every December and June for extended visits and feel as if we'd never left. Some people have well-branched families and love every leaf on the family tree. I do. That's probably why it seems quite natural to have two homes and care deeply for both.

Our summer visit to Michigan usually extends over a month. Then we try something new, test a new frontier. This past summer, we loaded Kodiak and our gear into the back of the new pick-up; Kodiak perched in style on the thick bed David had made on a shelf at box height. We continued our previous exploration of Wyoming and Montana, camping in remote forests or mountain meadows and awakening to the sound of sand hill cranes or freestone creeks. We'd hiked and fished our way into fall. Then we said our annual end of the summer good-byes in Michigan and journeyed home to Maine.

So much to discover, so many old friends to re-visit. Kodiak trotted ahead as we dropped out of the clearing toward the south. Delicate hay-scented ferns lined the pathway, just barely knee high. Their little branches were twisted slightly at the stem making the steps of wispy elfin staircases. Some were turning a pale yellow with the shortening days. Rising above them, the flat tables made by the bracken ferns were still dark green. Higher yet, the great plumes of the ostrich ferns were just starting to brown a bit. In the early spring, these are the ferns beginning life as fiddleheads, natural three-inch imitations of the head of a violin. In Maine, harvesting fiddleheads from the wetlands is a rite of winter's passage. They're steamed and served fresh with butter, or they're blanched and tucked away in the freezer to await winter's return.

The sun danced down the path as Kodiak stopped to inspect a scent maker, a royal fern, distinct branches adorned with individually placed emerald fronds an inch long. We passed our old canoe landing and turned west toward the Grass Dam, strolling down a carpet of still green bunchberry leaves, some topped with clusters of dried red berries the deer mice and partridges hadn't yet found. As if carefully placed by a master landscape artist, another high, feathery fern accented the bunchberries along the path. The interrupted fern rivals the ostrich fern in size, but its showy plume is interrupted with a few inches of brown part way up the stalk. Like the ostrich ferns, the individuals are arranged in a circle from which the plumes sweep upward, nearly to my height.

As we approached the dam, an explosion of water and sound told me that the black ducks were as shy as ever. Their hoarse noisy exit swept up nearly a dozen wood ducks as the blacks flew north. The woodies, too, burst out of the water and then followed, crying out the alarm. A bittern lost its nerve and fled. They all grow quite used to our absence from their private summer sanctuary. The water level should have been much lower, but the beavers had mitigated the effects of the late summer drought. The surface dimpled by my feet; small minnows and tadpoles were sipping air.

The Grass Dam is usually green with grasses and sedges. It was exciting to see it alive with late season wildflowers. Little spotted trumpets of orange jewelweed dangled from the taller plants along with pods just then swelling to the touch-me-not stage, awaiting dispersal. Near the jewelweed, the last of the little purple shooting stars with yellow centers, purple nightshade, decorated equally tall, deep green plants where tiny tomatoes were already forming. Closer to the water stood two varieties of white flower, the demure monks' or turtles' heads and the delicate, three petaled arrowheads. The white flowers had twins, perfect reflections looking back from the mirror surface of the dark water. Paradise.

Coming back to Maine after a summer on the road, one has to establish priorities. We unload the truck and unpack the perishables, but that's where we draw the line; it's unpack on a strictly as-needed basis and get out to examine the property. What's out, who lives where, and how high's the water? The important parts of life.

This year, we had other happy pre-occupations. David's mother had preceded us to Maine from Michigan and was staying nearby with his sister, Barb. We had purchased the next house north of ours just before we left in June, and, most importantly, the twenty-eight adjoining acres originally cut out of our land that went with it. We didn't want or need the buildings, but reuniting the two pieces of land was appealing, stream flowing into ponds back into stream again. The house had come with the acreage in an offer we couldn't refuse. With Dorothy and Barb willing to pitch in, it was housecleaning first, land exploration second. Or maybe third. We did have to go back to work.

The new house, the north house as opposed to our snug south house a hundred yards through the balsams and whispering white pines on a trail we'd just cleared, was hardly new. It was spacious and open, however, and had a wide deck facing west, overlooking the largest beaver dam and two of the ponds. The kitchen was ruled by a wood burning cookstove in addition to the modern appliances, and the basement had a walkout door beneath the big deck, two small rooms, and a larger room big enough for a rod shop.

David makes split bamboo fly rods, a craft which has captured us both. Once smitten with cane, it becomes a preoccupation which, at least for us, includes some of the best parts of life.

To make a bamboo fly rod, David begins with a twelve-foot culm of cane. The cane he uses is imported from the Tonkin region of China by Harold and Eileen Demarest, good and lively people who paused in their travels to celebrate Harold's ninetieth birthday with the bamboo rodmakers in Grayling last summer. The culm of cane is split lengthwise into long strips.

After straightening, the cross section of each strip is eventually shaped into a equilateral triangle so that six strips fitted together form a hexagon, like a pencil but longer. Once heat-treated, the strips are tapered on a form with a hand plane, thicker at one end, thinner at the other, so that the butt of the eventual rod will be much thicker than the tip. Six of the strips are glued together, the dried glue sanded off the outside, and the section is dipped into a tank of varnish and drawn out slowly, a shiny, beautiful rod blank.

Then it's sanded down again and re-dipped up to five times so that every pore is filled and every facet is breathtaking. The nickel-silver ferrules to join the tip to the butt, the guides and the tiptop for path of the line, the cork grip, and the reel seat come last, and, sixty to eighty hours after it was first split, the bamboo becomes a fly rod.

David's mom and sister are very supportive. We all toured the north house, and they offered advice and assistance on every aspect of cleaning and decoration but smiled patiently when we lost interest in the interior early and temporarily abandoned the project. The house needed to be cleaned, we'd have to add a woodstove and hearth, and then we'd worry about the rest. David had a rod to finish, and I had added to his list a waiting repair. Besides, before the last vestiges of summer faded, I had to do inventory.

Not your everyday inventory. I knelt down on the Grass Dam to check for frogs. Juvenile bullfrogs, two of them hanging in the glassy film, stared back. The decided ridge clearly defined their earlobes, or I couldn't have distinguished them from green frogs. I picked a long stem of grass to tickle the nose of the nearest one until it was provoked into biting, a trick that apparently works well on both ends of the season. It realized its mistake immediately and let go, gliding past purple monkeyflowers and disappearing among the long stalks of cattails.

On the other side of the Grass Dam, we turned north, Kodiak still in the lead. Like jewels on a string, our chain of ponds is smaller at the ends, biggest in the middle. The first pond, south of the Grass Dam, begins where the flowing Hilton Brook disappears into a tangle of alders and tiny beaver dams, then spreads wide. It covers about five acres. After the Grass Dam, the Big Pond fills a bay of drowned trees, the Valley of the Dead, then widens to form a small lake, about thirty acres. On the west side is Duck Cove, then Bull Moose Cove. The Big Pond is ringed with our wood duck nesting boxes, and two large beaver houses lie near the north end. The Big Dam creating the northern barrier runs one hundred feet or more, five feet above the downstream water, and drops into the pond right in front of the north house where there is another beaver lodge. After making a ten acre passage through the North Pond, the waters of the Hilton drop over the North Dam, roughly as long as the Grass Dam at the south end. This is new territory. The Last Pond is as small as the South Pond, but the last dam holding it back is tiny, only about twenty feet across. It releases the Hilton as a stream, cascading northward over a bed of gravel and watercress. South Pond, Big Pond, North Pond, Last Pond: the Hilton Brook necklace.

Heading north on the trail from the Grass Dam, Kodiak and I both examined fresh signs of snowshoe hares near a moss-covered stump decorated with gold thread, a small green plant that could be mistaken for clover or wood sorrel except that it grows secret roots of a brilliant gold. Under a towering white pine which had somehow escaped the logger's saw, moccasin-flowers, pink lady-slippers, had given way to swelled green, cylindrical seedpods. The club moss running through their garden looked like miniature pine tree candles on a string.

We dropped off our land at Hemlock Ridge, crossed the old stone wall which marks the boundary, and circled around behind Bull Moose Cove. The water protrudes from our largest pond into the adjacent woods, so a quick trespass on friendly territory is necessary to access our land on the other side of the cove and continue around the pond. Fresh moose tracks, a cow and a calf, led up the little side stream to the west, and we detoured to follow them. The tiny dams on the feeder stream were apparently too porous, or the drought while we were gone had been more severe than we realized. Instead of a flowing freshet, the stream was reduced to a series of receding pockets connected by a mere trickle. The pool of water had shrunken considerably in one of them and was thick with shiners awaiting the autumn rains. It was disconcerting. They were isolated, caught in a fishbowl, only a few feet from an escape channel to the pond.

When we crossed the Hilton at the north end of the chain of beaver ponds, I was amazed to find so much water still flowing. The tiny trout have the beavers to thank for these sparkling ripples. This was the new territory, property now ours to explore and steward. I poked about until dark, discovering an empty black duck's nest nestled against the trunk of a beech and the bright red fruit of a jack-in-the-pulpit in a small hidden meadow. I crept through the primitive looking plumes of tall sensitive ferns to catch sight of the bittern, briefly, before its return trip south to the Grass Dam. There was burweed along the shoreline, and the last few elderberries, but absolutely no beechnuts or hazelnuts.

Circuit completed, I arrived back at the house with Kodiak to find David bagging a newly completed rod, and we shared each other's news. Mine evolved into a philosophical, or, at least, meteorological dilemma over the trapped minnows. Did the sidestream dry back every year? Could the minnows survive the stress? The natural world is cyclic, to be sure.

We walked together each evening as the week progressed to the trill of the toads on Hemlock Ridge and fresh moose tracks in the soft sphagnum at the water's edge, side-tracking every night to check on the minnows' situation. The shrinking pool on the feeder stream was six feet across, then five, then four, and the little minnows seemed doomed.

We'd just returned one evening when the phone rang, Scott Chase, one of our favorite bamboo rodmakers and a Maine native. We could hear the excitement in his voice. Something was up. Could we rendezvous with his family, say on the Kennebec, on Saturday afternoon?

At the site of the impromptu rodmakers' gathering the next day, we all exchanged greetings: Scott and Marcia, baby Erich on the way, two-year-old Anna, David, and I. We'd been apart all summer. We were going to cast a new rod, a Dickerson 9016 taper, 9 foot 9 weight, from Scott's talented hands. A finely crafted piece, as is his usual. But there was more going on.

There is always something exciting about the first cast of a newly created bamboo fly rod, but sharing the first cast with special friends, friends who appreciate craftsmanship and friendship and basic values we share and hold dear, that's more like the last picnic of summer.

The rod cast long and well, and we snapped pictures and laughed, and relaxed watching little Anna in her birthday party dress make the long climb up on to the picnic table to offer her curious, fresh perspective on the shiny new rod. We smiled at the name perfectly lettered on one facet. The soon-to-be owner was another Mainer, George Herbert Walker Bush. Although we hadn't ever voted in his favor, it was interesting to see what a guy who could have anything would choose. Somewhere below us, hidden by the trees, the Kennebec flowed; an eagle soared scouting its waters. Its flight might have been a daily occurrence on the river, but, that day, we all stopped to watch.

On Sunday, we mowed our clearing and the new lawn next door before Kodiak and I slipped off down the trail and David set the new taper on the planing form. He brought out the strips for the butt section of a new rod, and Kodiak and I found a white flower we'd missed in our inventory. A front had gone through sometime over the weekend when our minds were elsewhere, and we felt the nip in the air. The minnow pool was almost dry; David and I decided to take a little positive action of our own.

To begin the new week, David brought home the dipping nets he loans to elementary teachers studying the wetlands. They are finely meshed with the hoop that spreads the net open bent flat on one side. This feature made them perfect for scooping shallow water finding dragonfly nymphs last spring and would be just what the doctor ordered for ailing shiners. Though slightly embarrassed that we were interfering with a cycle that is probably repeated at the end of every summer, we headed off to the feeder stream. As we liberated the prisoners, dark clouds gathered. With any luck, fall would bring immediate relief to their unseen comrades elsewhere, and winter would bring lots of snow. Snow, the real headwaters of all small streams.

In the North, the conventional wisdom holds that there are four seasons, and while that's hard to dispute, it's not exactly true. In reality, where perception often rules, there is some disagreement over the number of seasons between summer's end and its beginning the following year. Living on a secondary road, one that isn't paved, prompts belief in a fifth season, mud season, which lies between winter and spring. If getting stuck or having our road wash out bothered us, we'd probably fall into this group. Although, if those things bothered us, we probably wouldn't live here in the first place. A lobsterman once told us he enjoyed the hard work of pulling up his traps every single time because it was "wicked interesting" just to see what was inside, sort of like a birthday present. Roads during mud season are like that.

Similar to anglers who have two seasons, fishing (April first to October first) and waiting to fish (the other six months), we live on a two season cycle. For us, though, there is summer, when life is easy, and winter, when life is simplified, reduced to its most basic components: safety, warmth, shelter, and fun, family and friends, and quiet reminiscence. Actions and consequences. Appreciation of what is and what we have at other times. Reflection. The real test of a person's character is in how he or she responds when life is hard, not easy. Winter reveals our inner secrets, and it reveals secrets in the natural world obscured in the prolific confusion of summer. A single set of animal tracks becomes an event. Laying a packed snowshoe path becomes the sole activity of an entire afternoon. Popcorn in front of the fire becomes a special moment. And there is time for rodmaking, crafting a sweet grass into a functional work of art. Winter. Cane and simple truth.

The butt sections of the newest rod were nearing their final dimensions before I found time to pore through the field guides to identify the new flower. I admired the heap of fragrant shavings and examined the fresh beauty of the handcrafted cane. David examined my sketch of the little flower and served as consultant while I thumbed the guides and he bound the cane for the night. Nodding ladies' tresses, two votes. A small, wetland orchid. A fall orchid. Then we placed the sketch of our new discovery on the counter and fell asleep to the sound of the returning fall rains. Maybe the minnows would have been okay.

Repairs

"We were best friends before we were anything else, and we've managed to stay that way."

David stripped the thread and then the varnish off the ferrule that secures together the tip and butt sections of my bamboo fly rod while I tried to take full and apologetic responsibility for unseating the ferrule in the first place. I knew better than to twist my rod when breaking it down, and I knew better than to expect him to let me take the blame. Mine was the first rod he'd ever made, and he suspected he'd learned a few things since then which could have made it better. I doubted it; he's meticulous, always, start to finish. We decided to repair it together.

David and I do almost everything together. We were best friends before we were anything else, and we've managed to stay that way. We were worried, initially, that time would work to undo us, and we were so wary of the pitfalls and problems of other married couples that we slipped the ceremony in quickly and tried to ignore the fact that it ever happened, just in case marriage itself was the jinx. So far, so good. It's still the worse part of my day when events fall so that we're apart. I carry a two-way radio on solo walks with Kodiak so that I can let David know when there's a moose in Bull Moose Cove, and he can radio me if he needs an extra hand gluing up a blank.

We were keeping in contact by radio last summer in Wyoming when I pulled my rod apart. Our plan had been to dive back into the willows along the Tongue to taunt the cuttthroats, or vice versa. But sometime before dawn, an SUV had come through the cattle gate and, despite the wide open spaces, pulled up to park barely a doorswing from our truck. We listened from our sleeping bags as they pulled on their waders, four excited anglers with a mission, and we packed up for other waters after they'd disappeared toward the stream.

Just a mountain range to the southwest, high on a pass, was a creek we'd fished only once. A spring creek flowing across a high grassy meadow, we'd seen no one there, and there had been plenty of fish. Memories can exaggerate the truth, even shared memories, so we crossed our fingers and headed out. We'd also heard of threats to pave the access road and develop the pass and hoped we weren't too late. We weren't. It was better than we remembered.

The Wind River Mountains have always made a formidable obstacle for travelers. At one end, South Pass was used as passage west, and there are wagon train ruts and deserted gold mines in the area still. David and I have backpacked across the backbone of the Winds, the Continental Divide near Gannet Peak at Indian Pass. It was a sunny place to cool off from the climb and chip glaciers for snowcones with our ice axes. Once we'd fished the headwaters of the Green River, we'd hoped to find a way to pass through the range on the other end, a short cut north. We poured over maps and talked to the locals until we finally did.

It was David's turn to fish first. With the potential for both grizzlies and wolves in the area, Kodiak would have to be leashed, and that job fell to me. David led the way down the exposed slope, sneaking up on the first and biggest pool. From just above him, Kodiak in check, I could see down into the water. It was crystal clear, thirty feet across, and swarming with cutthroats. Big cutthroats. Wild fish. I stopped to silently cheer David on.

He pulled out some line before nearing the bank and double checked the knot on a Dave's grasshopper. He was using the Medved rod, a 7 foot 4-weight, with a silk line. There was no cover. If the fish were spooky, he'd have one good chance.

I was rooting for a monster cruising right along the bottom to out-snatch its fellows when the medium cutt above it attacked David's fly. The little rod bent with the strain, and Kodiak and I ran down to watch. All of the other fish had disappeared, and David was trying to release this one before it ran to every corner of the pool. It was difficult. Finally, we three measured and admired the cutt, Kodiak's favorite part, made sure it was rested, and watched it shoot under the bank. Seventeen inches, not bad for a small creek.

My dog-free turn was over quickly when I enticed a small brook trout out from under that same bank, and Kodiak and I decided to move downstream beyond David's next pool. I switched the radio on in case he had good luck.

Kodiak trotted ahead on his leash, and the meadow widened. I could see there were no real dog-hazards, and Kodiak couldn't see David to interfere, so I decided to let him run free. We had wandered a little far from the truck. An eerie sight materialized ahead in the path; even Kodiak side-stepped it. I bent down for a closer look: a sitting frog, dried, dead. It looked like it had been hopping and just stopped and dehydrated on the spot. A frog mummy. I poked it with my finger, and it fell over on its stiff little side in a fairly unearthly way, just as the radio crackled.

"See the storm?" David asked.

I wheeled around. I hadn't. Black thunderheads were coming fast, and lightning cracked between them. I called for Kodiak and was trying to run toward the truck and to leash him at the same time when the wind hit. I was still in my waders and vest, Kodiak was excited, and my bamboo rod was in my hand when the first huge drops pelted us. David had the tailgate down and the cap door flipped up and boosted Kodiak right in. I grabbed the tip and butt of my rod, pulled, then twisted hard. David never even said "I told you so". He's not only my best friend; he knew he could fix it. We'd wait for winter, though.

David pulled the unwrapped ferrule from my rod, examined it and the butt where it had been mounted, then showed both to me. It looked like the ferrule hadn't been fully seated, and there had been a small gap in the glue. That may be the second good reason to keep a first rod in the family, although most rodmakers I know are like David. They'd repair any rod they had made for life.

He used a pointed diamond file to dig the residual glue out of the deep inside base of the metal ferrule without scarfing its interior sides. There is a thought that epoxy joints should be smooth. Besides, scraping them might oversize the ferrule, making for a sloppy fit. While he cleaned the ferrule and the turned down portion of the cane butt, I mixed the epoxy, measuring resin and hardener into tiny cups and then stirring them together until I made epoxy taffy. David prepared wax paper on the floor beneath our work area, found the paper towels and white vinegar for the clean-up, and scouted for last minute problems and details.

The bamboo cooking skewer I used for mixing became his applicator. He coated the end of the butt thinly, extending only half the distance the ferrule would cover. The rest would be coated as he pushed the ferrule on, and a wrap of masking tape would keep the ferrule off the adjacent finish. He used the slender, pointed skewer to apply a little epoxy inside the ferrule itself, smearing it around with the stick. I jammed paper towels in all of my pockets so that the ends mostly protruded, turning myself into a human towel dispenser. We were ready.

David worked the ferrule on to the rod. He rotated the ferrule a little, making me smile when I remembered why it had come off, then held the butt horizontally and pushed the end of the ferrule against the leg of the workbench. He held the rod with both hands, taking care not to bend it, and waited. This is the part where the trapped air bubbles are supposed to escape with a distinct, satisfying 'pop'. They didn't. He twisted the ferrule a tiny bit. No pops. A few more tries, and he patiently called it off.

David pulled the ferrule free again and dropped it in a test tube full of acetone to clean it, and cleaned the end of the butt carefully with vinegar. I finished the butt and pulled off the masking tape, checking for residual epoxy that would ruin the shine of the varnish. Epoxy has a gooey sense of humor and gets anywhere it can.

We debated the late hour and another try until we decided to heat the little cup of epoxy a bit by lowering it into hot water. We hoped to be able to stir the glue into a thinner consistency. The heat would speed the hardening, so we couldn't waste any time. Precision rod repair drill team. That time, the epoxy popped twice, and, with a little coaxing, popped a third time, and the ferrule was seated. David decreased the pressure in his push, and the ferrule didn't slide itself back off: no air pocket acting as a piston.

I took over the pressure application while David carefully wiped the excess epoxy from the ferrule tabs. Then he slowly wrapped thin crafting wire around and around the tabs, securing the ferrule on the rod for the night. Wire doesn't leave fuzz on the tabs. The particular epoxy he uses, borrowed from the golfing industry, cures slowly and stays quite flexible. It also takes longer to dry, but we were in no rush. We still had a few preparations to make before the snows started, and it didn't look like I'd need the rod anytime soon.

Part of getting ready for winter is storing some things away, getting others things out. We don't tend to squirrel away much food; we always seem to be able to come up with enough, usually on the run. Instead, we stash the fishing and warm weather gear where we can find it again and hoist the canoes onto the cross arms of the canoe shed. We double check the roof supports for load bearing capacity and make sure the snow scoop and shovels are there where we left them. The toboggans we use for hauling firewood in winter are kept there, too, along with the wheelbarrow we use in the fall. Since David was going to tune up the snowblower, I headed for the woodpile.

The covered row of split wood stacked up along the driveway had been delivered two years earlier. We put down pallets and built cross-stacked towers at either end, then piled the rest of the full cord in between. Our home is mostly earth-bermed and we have a backup heat source, so we can enjoy a cozy fire in the evenings, stay warm, and use just a little wood or kerosene. Still, every stick has to be stacked after its delivery by the local guy who salvages treetops from the logging operations, then loaded and hauled to the door, and stacked again near the woodstove. We do a rack full every couple of weeks and enjoy it every time. At most, it takes an hour.

The progressing afternoon was warm, but the forecast said the evening would see rapid change. We decided to carry the big aluminum canoe, the most stable platform and the most weather worthy, down the hill to the biggest pond. This middle pond is nearly a half mile long and a quarter mile across. The canoe would be handy left on the immediate shore in case of trouble on the thin ice soon to come, but it would also make the best vehicle for detaching and retrieving our wood duck boxes.

When the beavers flooded the Hilton Brook into our series of small lakes, they didn't have the good fortune of the marine clay lining the Mercer Bog in the next valley. Their dams are more porous and need constant attention, and our wood duck boxes sink lower every year on the posts driven into to bottom. Six boxes had descended too low, three of them touching the water, so we loaded Kodiak in for the ride, grabbed an assortment of wrenches for the securing bolts, and paddled the big canoe out. It was a joy to be out on the water, albeit a bit chilly in late October.

October first fell on a Sunday, the day on which Maine practices universal armistice; there was no hunting that day. We're not duck hunters ourselves, but our life often seems to be intertwined with one. With all those who are immersed in the out-of-doors, environmentalists, conservationists, sportsmen, recreationists, there are no clear lines, and, in the end, partnerships and alliances are a way of life.

Our chain of ponds becomes a major stopover for ducks and geese each fall. Just as the summer's wood ducks fly south, dozens of ringnecks establish temporary residences, joined by assorted mergansers, teal, mallards, black ducks, and Canada geese. We marvel at them every autumn, spying from behind balsam fir and hemlock at the water's edge until we can steal a photograph or some video footage.

I could hear geese from our clearing and was waiting for the sun's angle to lengthen before slipping down to the water when Kodiak woofed an alert to another sound. David was preoccupied with the chainsaw, so Kodiak and I took the camera to investigate. A canoe was coursing down the length of the pond toward the geese; we could hear the hollow wooden sound as paddles tapping the gunwales moved progressively toward the flock. I ran through the trees in time to see our neighbor Chris and his brother, in all innocence, working their way to the beaver lodge. They're the only hunters who have permission to hunt here and were probably going to set up a blind. They came into view of the geese. The geese snapped to attention.

"Are you going to scare away those geese before I can take their picture?" I called out. Both paddlers froze. Then they looked my way and scanned the water to the north.

"Oh, no," I heard Chris groan, but he was drowned out by the sound of one hundred geese honking and taking flight. One hundred pairs of wings flew over the canoe. They banked to the south and flew back just over my head. I could hear the whoosh of each pair of wings as a regal dignity was regained. We all watched as the V disappeared to the north.

"Sorry," Chris called apologetically.

I was disappointed to lose both the photograph and the moment, but life necessitates trade-offs and compromise. Earlier this year, we mentioned to our close friend Janet that we'd just watched a movie about the legendary Grey Owl. She was patiently indignant.

"I don't watch movies about white guys pretending they're native Canadians and trapping beavers," she lectured us.

While both of her underlying points were true, Archibald Stansfeld Belaney went on to lay the foundation for modern conservation in that country and is credited with bringing the beaver back from near extinction.

As the conversation progressed late into that night, we mentioned that a professor, Cathy Bevier, and her students from a local college spent the summer studying mink frogs in our pond while we were away. We loved sharing our new discovery. Mink frogs, we told her, have a mottled, maybe defensive coloration, smell as bad as their namesake when handled, and are pretty much the northernmost frog. We were excited that our pond is within the limit of their range, an anomalous habitat in this part of Maine. Then we noticed the chill in the air.

"Are they going to kill the frogs?" she asked, certainly a good question. She can cut to the chase, no doubt about it. These are the conversations that good friends can have. They keep us all introspective.

"Well, yes," we admitted. "Maybe. We're not really sure. Maybe. A few." But we hastily explained that mink frogs have incredible reflexes despite their cold environs, and research into their biochemical makeup could contribute to the understanding of related afflictions. Maybe arthritis.

She wasn't buying it. "So animals have to die just to help humans?"

The stakes were higher than that, we told her, not mentioning that even Kodiak has his twinges. As long as the pond is a scientific study site, we have our own kind of ammunition to pencil in on the form which demands to know just why we want our property exempt from beaver trapping. In order to protect the beavers we inadvertently befriend by our close daily presence, we have to petition the State each year and include a sound rationale for our closure request. It's our fault they're habituated to humans; it's our responsibility to safeguard them in their misguided trust. The prolific mink frogs might trade a few of their number to save the animals which made the pond the minks live in.

With the flock of geese gone, Kodiak and I continued our walk along the shore. We circumnavigate the pond each evening; it takes about an hour. At the south end, Chris had parked his truck. His tailgate displays his politics with bumper stickers promoting children and fishing, restoring the American chestnut, and protecting wild Atlantic salmon. A registered Maine Guide, he is a member of the Kennebec Chapter of Trout Unlimited, the group that holds shared responsibility for the historic removal of the Edwards Dam on the Kennebec River against the owners' wishes. That TU also established a trout pond dedicated solely to use by children, future anglers and conservationists, and provides mentors to teach my students each spring. They are regulars in the middle school library media center where I enjoy a daily immersion in the wonders of pre-teenagers and all the world around them.

On the far side of the pond, Kodiak and I again made our way down through the hemlocks to the shore. From there, I could see where the geese had been and directly across to where I stood to call out to the canoeists. Two years ago, I had stood in that same spot and tried in vain to call out to three men across the pond, trespassers with guns. The goslings we had watched hatch from the nest on the beaver lodge had grown into five beautiful copies of their parents, geese I'll always admire for their determined dedication. Even during tremendous thunderstorms, we had seen them illuminated in silhouette by the lightning, sitting on top of the house protecting those eggs. But all seven geese were swimming between my position and the poachers, who were pulling up their guns. I realized that they didn't care that the land was posted. They didn't care that there was no goose season in Maine that year, that shooting geese was a felony.

The seven geese saw the movement of the guns and rose from the water crying to each other. I yelled and yelled through the flapping of wings and the doomed honking and saw the guns point in my direction as they tracked the geese flying by. I can still hear the sound of them firing and see the two geese fall into the water.

The poachers suddenly saw me across the pond, and, running into each other like stooges, dropped their shells and ammunition and fled into the woods, abandoning the two fallen geese.

Shaking the memory off, I could also see Chris and his brother now from that same shore. They had constructed a blind near the site of the nest on the lodge and were dropping decoys into the water. In exchange for hunting, Chris patrols the pond. Last year he asked two trespassers on the same spot as their predecessors to reassess their location. We know that Chris is well-known and respected; his presence is really all it takes. As for the ducks, he usually only takes two, just enough for a couple of dinners and a good supply of feathers for tying flies. Some of those flies go toward ensuring that the next generation loves and respects the outdoors too.

Chris saw me on the shore.

"We put the blind on the beaver house. We should get some tail slaps in the morning when they find us," he called, adding,

"Sorry about scaring off the geese."

"That's okay," I said, sincerely. "I'm just glad you could enjoy them, too."

"We sure did," he called back.

I knew both that he meant it and that there are no simple answers in any ecosystem.

David and I were covered with wet duck box bedding but still having fun by the time we finally made it back to shore with the six remarkably heavy boxes, and Kodiak jumped on to the hummocks near the shore. I pulled the canoe up, and we unloaded and washed it out before flipping it over and leaning it against a balsam fir. Stacked nearby were the twelve concrete blocks I'd lugged down, one at a time, that we planned to use to make a rack which would support the canoe above the first few snows. After that, the ice would be so thick that a ready rescue canoe wouldn't be as crucial. Then we carried the wood duck boxes up to the canoe shed, one by one.

We had just enough afternoon left to load up the snowblower and take it to town. The secondary stage impeller was bent, and we wouldn't be throwing snow without having it straightened. The inclement weather forecast was accurate, and the temperature dropped steadily, even with clouds moving in. Sometime, amid unloading the snowblower in town and grabbing something to eat on the way back out, winter began. The first snow. It started as a few flakes we weren't sure we'd really seen, and intensified into the first real accumulation, admittedly more beautiful to enjoy at home than to experience on the road.

By the time we returned to greet and liberate Kodiak, we'd spent nearly an hour in a long line of nervous drivers crawling through three inches of slush. The snow had started as sleet which froze on windshields and wipers. Caution lights flashed as cars pulled on to what hopefully was shoulder, not ditch, to clear windows and steady nerves. The slow speed didn't bother us. The temperature would continue to fall with the darkness, and a greasy commute was worth the first real snowfall of winter. We passed a slightly embarrassed car which had slid off the shoulder and was finding its way back.

Before reaching home, we stopped briefly at the north house. The mason would be out soon to start the brick chimney. It would extend from basement to roof, with a hearth and mantle in the living room. With two flues, we'd be able to have a woodstove in the basement as well as the living room to complement the wood cookstove in the kitchen. We had stacked a rack full in that basement already. For the meantime, we turned up the furnace a bit to compensate for the onset of winter.

Our own little south house on the other side of the firs was outlined in the night when we arrived. The full moon was masked by the moody clouds, but still reflected enough light off the new snow so that we could see. Kodiak romped around, greeting us and rejoicing in winter. He was born in October and spent his formative months in deep Maine snow. Along with those suspected husky genetics, I've always thought his first few months of life must have made a lasting impression. I had been born in October, too.

David inspected the ferrule repair and pronounced it a success. He would dab epoxy between the tabs next, then smooth it even with their height; otherwise, even if tabs are feathered, small air pockets could form which would look white when varnished under thread. He'll wrap the tabs in fine, clear silk, and then layer it with coats of varnish. He was looking up his notes on the thread he'd previously used when I went back out to persuade Kodiak to come inside.

The snow had stopped, and the night had been transformed. Our roof, decks, and windowsills were blanketed in white, illuminated in the snowblue light of the moon. The night had retreated; every far-reaching corner of the clearing was bathed in a bluish white glow.

Kodiak, exploring by moonlight balsam firs laden with snow, had tangled in dark green-black branches hung low, heavy, and blue-white. I freed him and brushed the snow off his back, then stepped on to the snow-covered deck and leaned against the cedar shingles near the door, thinking how peaceful it all was. I could see David working inside through the warm light of the window.

The Odds

*"The question hurt:
How close could I get
to the struggling dog."*

I wonder, sometimes, if my luck just might run out. One of these winters, for instance, what if... ? That in mind, I've always believed that there is risk in everything, that some of us trade one risk (say, traffic or urban violence) for another (say, a blizzard or falling through the ice), and that the accompanying danger can be mitigated. Do what you can and go on enjoying life. Forewarned, forearmed, not alarmed. Still, the odds could be stacking against me, depending on how you look at it.

Kodiak has fallen through the ice twice that really counted. All the other incidences were relatively minor, and he scrambled out under his own power. It's impossible to avoid ice entirely if you're in Maine in the winter. There's water everywhere; that's why we like it. We could keep him constantly on a leash; we could just lock him in the house and force him to live life through a window. We compromise by keeping him tethered when he's outside alone, leashing him when there's a hazard, and accepting our role as watchful eye when we're all off for a good jaunt.

Once in mid-December, Kodiak fell through the ice of Bull Moose Cove and hung up on a submerged log. David and I

41

devised a hasty plan where I would wade out into the pond, the ice being thin, while he wrestled down a small tree to use as a rescue pole, if necessary. Going first was mostly my idea; it seemed wiser to save the strongest for the last ditch effort. We weren't really sure what wading in ice water would be like; hopefully, only one of us would need to find out. It was rather chilly but not impossible in the shallow water of the cove.

The second time Kodiak fell through had been two years later in early March. He was in very deep water and rotten ice surrounding the biggest beaver lodge. We were snowshoeing and had to resort to a variant of the same plan. That time, though, the ice was covered with a foot of ice water, and the wade out was frigid but not nearly as cold as dropping through a hole into the pond would be. I decided to wear my snowshoes to disperse my weight. David pulled his off in case that turned out to be a bad idea, and snowshoes worked more like anchors in the water. Then he wrestled down another rescue tree.

We were both quite apprehensive as I shuffled farther from shore, but there was no choice. Kodiak was terrified. He couldn't get any purchase on the lip of the hole and his eerie howl still haunts my worse dreams. Maybe he shouldn't have gone out to the beaver lodge, but we were equally responsible for not leashing him around the ice. We are usually considered to be the more sentient beings. We had thought leashing would be too confining; we had probably been wrong. Actions and consequences. I waded carefully out.

It took forever. When I was finally within calming distance, I tried talking to Kodiak while I inspected the ice a foot down below the surface of the meltwater. Small floating icesheets and drifts of slush would block my view, and I would have to sweep them away with my soggy wool mitten to view below. As nearly as I could tell, it was like snowshoeing over Swiss cheese. David and I conferred on what I was seeing, and he waded out to get into position to reach me quickly with the uprooted fir should what seemed inevitable ultimately happen. My stomach felt sick, and I talked to Kodiak to keep us both levelheaded.

The question hurt: how close could I get to the struggling dog? The ice obviously gave at sixty pounds. Where was the line at one hundred? He was so close; all that was left between us was a three-inch stump, like a little island amidst a two-foot wide barrier of questionable ice. I was stopped. I couldn't step up on it, too little for any kind of balance, especially with only one foot and snowshoes. I didn't dare take the shoes off since, for all I knew, they were holding me up. I put my hand on the stump, testing it. Very solid. Solid enough to lean on. I reached over the stump with my other hand, a little like doing a one-armed push-up with a decided adrenaline assist, and touched Kodiak. David reminded me to put my hand on the back of his head, a technique useful for helping him up into a canoe in the summer, and Kodiak immediately arched his back and neck. Using my hand for resistance leverage, he pulled himself out. He bounded through the meltwater and on to the lodge to shake off.

There's no way to backtrack a route that's across submerged ice, so David stood ready on shore with Kodiak until I found a safe path. After that, we changed our ways. We didn't stop hiking on or near ice; instead, we always carry an ice axe, rope, and dry clothes. What we don't carry is a grudge against the pooch.

In truth, Kodiak hadn't been the first one of us to have trouble falling in cold water. David had led the way. He's always much more willing to push the envelope than I am, and therefore always advances farther faster. I eventually get to nearly the same point but try to minimize the personal injury parts of skiing, ice skating, ice climbing, hang gliding, and the like, just a bit more than he does. If there are odds that something will happen to one of us, especially if it involves learning something new, I'll bet on David every time.

The trouble with late November is that it has both perfectly sunny days and canoes which go on sale. Some would say that we have plenty of canoes. We have, over time, collected a racing tandem, a rugged aluminum Grumman for fishing and tending wood duck boxes, an Old Town square stern (with oars), and maybe a couple others. The answer to that old canoeing question, 'how many canoes do you need?' is 'one more'. Different canoes for different functions, sign of flexible individuals or canoe junkies.

So when a used kevlar solo came up for sale one November, the day was of the too-sunny-for-your-own-good variety that tweaks away any inhibitions, and, in a fit of spring fever, we bought the canoe. How can we improve our skills if we don't push the envelope? We loaded it gingerly and didn't even bother to go home. November days are too short. David's sister Barb and our then brother-in-law lived on the way to the Mercer Bog, beautiful canoe water, and they had paddles and cushions. We stopped to share our excitement and borrow some gear. The Bro and a visiting student decided to drive over to watch the maiden voyage.

David, of course, went first. I certainly wouldn't have had it any other way. The canoe had a high pedestal seat and a deep, racing V hull; I thought I'd be as unwieldy astride it as David looked, although he countered that, at least, my center of gravity would be about a foot lower. We threw in the cushions and pushed him off. The water sparkled in the sunlight, diamonds in the breeze, and we ran along the shore, laughing with him and joking as he mastered the new canoe.

Then he turned to paddle back.

Probably he was just too tall and leaned too far to one side. It happened so quickly I couldn't be certain. There was a sudden splash, the extra paddle and the cushions scattered, and the canoe skittered away. David re-surfaced and let out a big whoop. We had frozen for a minute, watching from the west shore, and then we all laughed, and the student clapped his hands at the surprise.

"It's cold!" David yelled.

We stopped laughing. It was November. I dropped to feel the water. Too cold; icy cold. I clicked on the timer of my watch.

"He can't swim in this cold," I said.

"I'll go get my canoe." The Bro grabbed his sidekick and ran for his truck.

I never took my eyes off David. He had abandoned his paddle and reached out to grab a cushion. He wrapped his arms around it and held the cushion's insulating buoyancy to his chest. His muscles locked with the cold, and he couldn't let go.

I noticed that the light wind had hidden strength, blowing the canoe farther away from David. What were the options?

"David, are you okay?" I called out. I glanced at my watch. It had only been two minutes.

"Yeah, it's just cold," he said. He was wearing a light nylon windbreaker, cotton t-shirt, jeans, and tall rubber boots.

"Can you kick over to me?" I asked.

He tried, but couldn't. I hoped it would warm him a bit just from the effort of trying. It had been four minutes, and there was no sign of a rescue.

"I'm not getting anywhere, am I?" he asked. "Maybe my clothes have too much drag." He tried some more, splashing, getting his head wetter, colder. Six minutes. He was attracting some attention back at the road. Cars were stopping. People have drowned in Mercer Bog.

"I can't seem to get anywhere," he observed, characteristically calm and logical. He stopped kicking. Actually, between his movement and the wind, he was getting farther away.

"Just don't let go of the cushion," I yelled out. "I'll run around to the other shore."

"I won't," he promised. He sounded so calm.

I ran to the road, now lined with cars. "What's happening?" voices asked.

"He fell out of a canoe," I panted to all of them. Who would help? I had to hurry. Twelve minutes. "He can't swim in that cold water."

"I'm a lifeguard," a quiet voice offered. "Maybe I can help."

A lifeguard driving by? What were the odds? I think I grabbed the hand and focused on the voice on the way down the other shore while spewing forth the details, including the time. Fourteen minutes. It must have made an impact because he took to the water before we were even with David. Maybe swimming would be faster. I pushed through the brush at a spot nearest David, still so far from shore. He was happy, though.

"It's not so cold anymore," he called over when he saw me.

"You've been in the water so long you're probably getting hypothermic. Don't let go of the cushion. You don't know how cold you are." I looked for the lifeguard. "Help is on the way." My heart broke. The lifeguard had turned back.

I scanned the water for the rescue canoe. Nothing. I looked the other way for our new canoe, the other cushion, anything. I would need some flotation. But, maybe, if he had his cushion, maybe I could swim out. I swim pretty well, and we're both fairly thin. Could one cushion get us both back? I wrestled with the problem until I looked at my watch. I was dropping my jeans when the lifeguard stepped out of the brush beside me.

"Too cold to swim that far," he said. Would he try it again? David interrupted.

"Look," he called out, happily. "My boots are pulling me to shore." The lifeguard and I looked at each other, slightly dumfounded.

"What?" I called out.

"If I extend my legs and jerk them toward me, the water catches in the boot, and I think it's pulling me forward."

"Okay," I said to the lifeguard. "Now he's lost his mind. I'm going to go get him."

He grinned. "I'm going. Think he'll pull me under?"

I suddenly became aware of two things. I was asking a stranger to risk his life, and my pants were half off. I looked down to zip up and spotted a length of twine at my feet. Amazing.

"Sorry. How about this?" I gave him the rope and my sincerest reassurance. "Listen to him, he's not at all panicked. And he doesn't bite."

He took the twine and swam out. I think he was persuading happy David that he really didn't mind and they should probably talk back on shore when the Calvary shot past them in the rescue canoe at nineteen and a half minutes. The tow to shore was in progress by the time the canoe turned around, so the other cushion, paddle, and new canoe were rescued instead.

The lifeguard disappeared into a swarm of protective arms, and someone handed me a dry shirt for David. As soon as he left the water and the pain of thawing hit him, his smile vanished. The soft flannel of the shirt hurt his skin and burned him, he said. We walked back through a gauntlet of well wishers, and I loaded him into the passenger seat of our truck. Everything hurt him. I would have raced home, but he wouldn't let me shift out of first gear. He said we were going too fast.

People who have been immersed in cold water might seem relatively fine at first once they're out, but I'd heard about "after drop," the term for the cold blood pooled in the arms and legs starting to circulate again when the victim starts to warm. It super-cools the heart and can be fatal. I wasn't going all the way home, no matter what he wanted.

I pulled into Barb's house to peel him free of wet clothing and put him in bed. He complained that the down comforter was too heavy and the cocoa she made with cool tap water was too hot. A shadow lifted from his face and his spirits as he approached 98.6 degrees, and we knew he'd be okay. He found the telephone to call his rescuer to say thanks and make sure he, too, was all right. We measured the temperature of Mercer Bog the next day. Forty-two degrees.

It was two years later before we found out that our lifeguard, by then a neighbor, had a terrible life-threatening heart condition. A true, selfless hero. He never brings it up; accidents happen. But we'll never forget.

As for the odds that my own luck will run out, I still wonder. Barb also preceded Kodiak with her cold water borderline disaster, although, in her case, the water was frozen and she didn't fall through. Falling on the ice on her head might actually hurt worse the next day than taking a dunking, judging more by David's calm response than Kodiak's panic. So of the four of us, Barb, David,

Kodiak, and I, that just leaves me. Wet twice but never truly fallen in. I don't really worry about it, just prepare as best I can and go out and enjoy winter. I wonder though, what are the odds? Maybe three out of four? Statistically, I'd be immune. Sort of. On the rodmakers' list serv at the onset of winter there was discussion about winter fishing, practicing falling on ice-slickened rocks, and the like. I read it all. I think it's probably safest just to assume that I could be next and then put it in the back of my mind and head outside.

To Leash or not to Leash?

"The only way to completely avoid risk is to avoid life, which pretty much defeats the purpose."

In a remarkable showing of tremendous support, my colleague-turned-principal Jennifer Haney asked my superintendent to grant me three weeks leave to delve into winter, and he agreed. The weeks I chose were those adjoining the holiday vacation, so I'd have thirty-eight days of personal and professional bliss, a once in a lifetime opportunity for a middle school librarian. I celebrated the first morning by waving David off at six, then loading Kodiak in the car and heading to Barb's for breakfast with Dorothy.

When David and I were first married, we called his parents to share the news. Dorothy was worried she'd be a bad mother-in-law, but nothing could be farther from the truth. That she was visiting Barb for the length of my leave was a glad coincidence. Kodiak and I planned to stop in, only a mile north on the way to town, then run for groceries and beat the impending storm home. A big snowstorm with heavy winds was in the forecast and had been for a couple of days. Barb, David, and I had related all sorts of power outage stories to Dorothy, so they were very much on her mind. Barb's, too, as it turned out.

Dorothy met us at the door and welcomed us in with a smile about something. Kodiak trotted over to the treats cupboard and sat as regally as he could muster until she offered him one, making him choose between two clenched outstretched hands by swatting the one holding the prize with his foot.

"Which one?" she asked; he swatted right the first time. She turned to me, still grinning. "Did your electricity go out last night?"

I was amazed. The storm hadn't arrived, and the night was calm. "Nope. Did yours?"

"No," she laughed, "but we thought it had".

Dorothy had awakened mid-night in cloud shrouded darkness in a pitch black house. She used her flashlight to rouse Barb in the other bedroom, and they made their way downstairs together to find a corded telephone. With groggy clarity they realized that the cordless phone in the bedroom wouldn't work without power. They rummaged around for the emergency number and called the power company.

"What time did your power go off?" the voice asked.

Barb didn't know, so she flipped on the light switch and read her watch.

My mother-in-law and sister-in-law can both take a joke, even at their expense. They're cut from the same classy but durable cloth.

The snow held off still. When we were back from town and lunch was over, I decided to slip in a good walk with Kodiak. There was a basic question to consider, though, while I geared up. Should I leash him or not? Leashing was the safest option if basic operator comfort wasn't a consideration. He'd more or less drag me along unless I constantly nagged him, something I never like to do with dogs or humans. He wouldn't get much of a walk, either, compared to the distance he'd travel retracing his steps and investigating every nook and cranny while waiting for me to catch up. On the other hand, leashing him all but guaranteed he'd be safe.

David and I had been carrying a 100 foot rope on our walks together since the ice had frozen just solid enough to fool Kodiak into thinking it was safe but not solid enough to guarantee us his weight, all sixty pounds of him, would be supported. At least, not uniformly. Our theory was that if he fell through (again), this time I'd loop one end of the rope around my wrist before going after him, and David could rescue us both.

Walking Kodiak alone was a different matter. We had talked it over a couple of times and come up with a few ideas, and I'd discussed alternative approaches to the problem in the hallway with my friend Joey on my last day at school. Math people love this kind of problem. Would I tie off to a tree, lasso Kodiak, or walk a wide circle around him and extract him somehow? We didn't really solve it, but additional objective input helps, and the conversation is always interesting.

Kodiak wagged and whined with impatience while I pulled on my boots. He has a way of arching his ears and wrinkling up his brown widow's peak that is very puppy-like. One ear was flipped over backward, cream colored side up. I flipped it back over for him, and he flopped into his 'lay down' stance to be even more endearing. He has a bivisible color scheme, golden brown from above, cream colored if viewed from below. His face is cream, but a brown widow's peak comes down in a point over his forehead, like an earthtone husky. He virtually disappears standing in a sunny autumn leaf pile.

I was stalling a little, weighing the odds. Was there anything else I could do to mitigate any risk? The only way to completely avoid risk is to avoid life, which pretty much defeats the purpose.

I tied his florescent scarf loosely around his neck and snapped his collar over it so the scarf couldn't slip off. He'd be visible under the heavily laden trees. The snow from the last storm still bent everything low, and I knew it would muffle sounds – me calling him, him barking, the jingle of his dog tags. Maybe I'd be able to spot his orange scarf.

I grinned and pulled on my bright red jacket.

"If we both go in," I told Kodiak, "at least David will be able to see us frozen in the ice."

Kodiak was ready, so ready. I looked out the window as I picked up his leash. There were snowshoe hare tracks across the clearing and red squirrel tracks under the feeder. I weighed them in on the side of no-leash. The land was potentially more interesting than the ice. What about mink? My heart tried to steer me to the safest path, but my head knew that mink smells, objects of obsessive fascination for Kodiak, were most likely in the dams or on pond banks.

I coiled his new leash and slipped most of it into my back pocket. The clip end I pulled free and snapped it to a beltloop so I wouldn't lose it. I had learned a lesson from some Wyoming willows.

"Okay, but don't get into trouble," I told Kodiak looking him right in the eye. He play-bowed back. I opened the door, and he was off like a maniac after the feeder squirrels. I could be in trouble, I thought, heading out after him.

I called Kodiak off the scolding red squirrel up the maple, and we both dropped down out of the clearing on the path to the south. The snow had fallen early Saturday, but winds never came, so it stayed on every twig, every fir needle. The dark green fir boughs were once again laden in white, but I couldn't remember them ever being more beautiful. Take-your-breath-away beautiful.

The snow covered firs encircled the entire pond, accenting the dark new ice. The pond had frozen just after the last snowfall, and the ice was so transparent the black water showed through. Black ice ringed with white. Under today's stormcast, the snow in the woods was brighter than the milky sky. There would be no starlight tonight.

By the looks of the sky, we were in a three-day pattern. The evidence of the last storm would still be around when the next one arrived. It seemed imminent. On the trail, the snow was almost fluffy, about four inches deep. It didn't scatter as I walked through it, but it wasn't crusty, either. It looked like vanilla frosting. Good tracking snow.

As we neared the Grass Dam, I was relieved to see Kodiak sticking to the trail. The hole in the ice half way across the dam was obvious but frozen over. Kodes had fallen in just yesterday, but it had been warm and sunny, and he'd been close to the dam. He had pulled himself out, shook, and had gone about his duties unperturbed and unharmed. I hoped one good early lesson would save us both some grief later on.

I paused after the Grass Dam to look over some young trees growing from stump sprouts the beavers had left behind. Two inches of heavy snow had outlined gray maple branches and adhered so tightly that when gravity worked its magic, the ribbons of white had stayed intact but twisted around the tree's long finger-like limbs, spiraling into hanging garlands. Kodiak waited while I stopped to shake some birch saplings free of snow. They were so heavily laden that they bent all the way to the ground and blocked the path. If the coming storm turned to sleet, the extra weight would snap the trunks. I remembered the sound from the Ice Storm a few years before.

Kodiak and I kept to the higher hemlock covered ridge, and then dropped into the big pines behind Bull Moose Cove, veering away from the pond. I decided to follow the linking trail to the snowmobile trail, the old summer road up Hampshire Hill. Kodiak paralleled me, inspecting the dams on the side stream. I looked over to check the ice of the minnow pool for the telltale signs of seeped water. It seemed dog-solid, and Kodiak by-passed it, anyway, keeping to the streambank.

The snowmobile trail had not been traveled yet this season, wise considering we had had only four inches of snow. Maybe after tonight, but for now it was unused. We decided not to use it either. I glanced at my watch. I had started out at two; it gets dusky at four. We should be able to make it up the west ridge and loop back with time to spare. Kodiak saw me glance right and ran ahead down the trail. I whistled to stop him and pointed across the road up the ridge. There was an old trail hidden beneath the snow, but he'd traveled it with us before.

"That way," I called, and he bounded into the woods and up the ridge, leading his pack.

We had started working on Kodiak's vocabulary right after he moved in. Some words he obviously needed to know, some evolved along the way, and others were just for fun. 'No' and 'come here' were givens. 'This way' and 'wait' came up on our first walks. 'Drop it', implying 'over there' as opposed to 'give' meaning 'bring it to me over here', became an obvious need when he found a very dead, dripping ripe mouse and in puppy exuberance wanted me to have it. David taught him to translate the former into action while I sat with my head between my knees, recovering. 'Find David', or 'Kathy', started as a means to locate one another utilizing Kodiak's sharp nose but came in handiest when David dropped the car keys on a lawn where we were enjoying hometown fireworks on the 4th of July. The next day, Kodiak found the keys in the expansive elementary school yard. 'Shake' and 'which one', which fist has the treat, were easy games he could play with the nieces and grandparents.

Deadfalls obscured the way to the top of the ridge, but there were none I couldn't go around or over, none that Kodiak couldn't go under. We panted to the top, then headed north until we intersected an old stone wall. It was laid up New England style, four feet wide at the base and nearly as tall as I. Climbing over it to the side with the larger, older pines and less underbrush, I turned east to follow the wall back down the side of the ridge. I'd have less snow to brush off my hat and shoulders. Kodiak stuck to the bunny trails on the side with all of the underbrush, and we met at the old spring holes at the base. From there, it's a short scramble to the granite stones of the old Kimball Mill Site and on to the snowmobile trail. We emerged north of our linking trail back to the pond, so we turned south toward it, and Kodiak took off on a dead run. He knows when we're heading home.

I stopped near the huge granite blocks of the old barn foundation to readjust my wool socks on the even ground of the snowmobile trail and to enjoy the beauty of gray-black granite draped in snow. There had once been two large barns, one with a walk-out lower level for the cattle, one with a granite-bermed ramp leading to the main floor, maybe for driving a buggy in or accessing the hayloft. A smaller shed had been nearby, its foundation made of cobblestones, maybe a chicken house, and the phantom house was outlined near the disappearing road. There was a stone lined cistern ten-feet deep in the back yard. It had been a long time ago.

The trees had grown tall, even in the center of the old foundations.

Kodiak raced on ahead and was nowhere to be seen when I looked up from my boots. I assumed he'd wait at the head of the linking trail, just to make sure I was turning, and I continued on expecting to meet him there.

At the linking trail, he was still nowhere in sight. I tried calling him and waited. I wasn't too concerned when he didn't come; the snow burdened branches muffle every sound. Maybe he couldn't hear me. We've walked that trail hundreds of times; he knew the way too well and could be waiting for me to catch up somewhere more interesting. I knew I'd catch up with him. I hoped he was very tired from the slog around the loop. I thought maybe I would leash him to go back around the pond.

I called to him and whistled all down the linking trail, passed the ice-covered minnow pool, all along the stream. I didn't really look for him since the bent trees and drooping boughs made visibility difficult, hiding even orange bandanas, but I kept an ear open. I thought I'd find him at the pond. I didn't.

At the end of the linking trail, Bull Moose Cove comes into view, but, until the ice is solid, we always veer south through the big pines. Kodiak could have gone out, but I scanned the cove, aware of the weight of the long rope I was carrying, and there was no sign of him, no orange speck on the black ice. At least, not that I could see. I ducked into the pines and tried hard to see dog tracks. They might have been visible as distinct southbound prints over my earlier northbound ones, but there were so many layers of tracks from previous hikes sheltered under the pines that it was hard to tell.

"He's probably digging for mink at the little streamlet just before the hemlocks," I told myself.

The pines are separated from our property by a tiny stream, really a long beaver channel, and the remnants of a stone wall. I left the big trees and stepped on the marshy grass to cross the streamlet. There were no breaks in its ice. The only mink tracks were old, frozen in the slush of the day before. I crossed the stones and stepped on to Hemlock Ridge. I called Kodiak. Nothing. I looked down the side trail to Bull Moose Cove. Kodiak had fallen through the ice for the first time there. It was also the week before Christmas, and the water was very cold during the rescue. If I called out, and he was still back behind the pines, he might cross Bull Moose Cove as a short cut. I could just imagine it; he'd be safe, but I'd call him, and then he'd fall in. There were no tracks leading down the side trail to the cove, but he could have traveled under the brush. It seemed I had no choice but to quietly slip down there and scan the ice. The biggest, deepest part of the pond is visible from that shore. I was starting to worry.

It was a relief to leave Bull Moose Cove without a dog sighting. I climbed back up to Hemlock Ridge and paralleled the pond, heading south on the trail to the Grass Dam. No fresh tracks, but I thought Kodiak would take the bunny trails back. I was disappointed when I finally arrived at the Grass Dam. No Kodiak.

What to do now?

I knelt to inspect the dam. Too many layers of tracks; Kodiak could have gone on ahead. Not likely, though. Not his habit. He'd just as soon wait at the dam, prime mink territory. I turned to look north where the water flows from the dam widening into the pond through the barren, drowned trees we call the Valley of the Dead. No sign of a little brown dog. There was no choice but to go back and look for him. I checked my watch. Better run.

I stopped to catch my breath and listen on Hemlock Ridge. I called out once. Then I heard one bark, a 'come here' bark. One. It was muffled through the trees, and I couldn't even tell which direction it came from. The silence was oppressively heavy. Was it a come-see-my-new-hole bark or a help-me-out-of-the-water bark? In Bull Moose Cove that time, he'd been so hung up under water that he couldn't bark at all. I ran on, dropping down over the stones, crossing the streamlet, and into the Pines, formulating a plan. Call when in a safe place, where Kodiak wouldn't be tempted to cross the ice. Stop and inspect the pond from all vantage points. Listen for dog tags (I took off my hat). Stay logical, keep with the plan, be systematic. Go as fast as possible.

I rounded the cove where the linking trail begins just as snow started to fall and made my way to high hummock, a muskrat house, where I could see the far beaver lodge. The snow came down hard, blurring my vision and immediately turning the ice white. I scanned the pond for a black hole. Just north of the far house, in the deepest water, there was a hole, and something was in it.

I watched, my heart pounding. Stay calm. Make sure of what you see. Don't go out on the ice unless you're sure you can save Kodiak and yourself. It was the right size, but the dark shape was too calm, too dark. I watched it to be sure. A beaver.

"Kodiak!" I called, and then whistled hard into the woods. It was a small sound in a forest of white, sound-dampening firs. The storm intensified.

I followed the side stream toward the snowmobile trail, paralleling the linking trail this time along what I thought might be a dog route. The snow was starting to mask everything, and it was difficult going. Beaver traps had been set along this trail, just off our land. Still, if Kodiak was in one, I thought he'd make it known.

If he could bark once, I hoped, he couldn't be under water. A leg hold trap would hurt. I had heard Kodiak's terror-bark before, the second time he fell through the ice, out in deep water. No one could forget a bark like that.

If he was somewhere along the stream, I found no sign of it. He's probably digging for a mink somewhere, I told myself. He's fixated and acting like a jerk. I wasn't reassured much; where was he? Then I looked at my watch and heard myself cry out. Four o'clock. Dark in ten minutes.

I stifled my panic into a more rational frustration and re-formulated my plan. Run home, get a headlamp and two-way radio, call David at work and let him know what was happening. Then head back into the dark until he radioed for a rendezvous and, barring better luck in the meantime, a joint search. Remember to ask him to promise, I thought as I ran, promise not to go out on the ice alone. I thought that, realizing I might have done it if I thought I had a chance to save Kodiak.

I ran through the falling snow toward home with my hat and mittens in one hand, the rescue rope in the other, hair wet but free to listen as the dark closed in. The snow sizzled as it fell, sleet. It turned the dusk toward darkness and completely hid all my tracks. I crossed the streamlet in a running leap, trying to beat the darkness, climbed up to Hemlock Ridge, and ran south toward the Grass Dam. The trail had been wiped clean in front of me, clear except there was now one new set of tracks. Kodiak's. He was headed for the Grass Dam, too.

I ran after him as fast as I could. I thought I could fly. I nearly lost control running down the ridge, and I stopped just short of the dam. No Kodiak.

What?

I knelt down. The darkness and the snowstorm made it hard to look for tracks. None.

Then I heard the jingle. Dog tags! I turned and made out a bright orange scarf bouncing down the trail towards me. Kodiak came bounding up, then yiped in pain, and started rubbing his head on the ground. He pawed at his mouth. Something was wrong.

I dropped my hat, mittens, and rope, and felt for his leash. I unsnapped it from my beltloop and clipped it to his collar. He calmed a bit. I was taking over, the alpha.

"Let me see," I said. He let me look into his mouth for just a moment, then remembered his pain and pawed and rubbed his muzzle frantically. It was too dark to see porcupine quills, and I had no tools to pull any out, so we were up to Plan Three. Kodiak seemed to be breathing okay, and his feet and chest looked fine. Maybe the roof of his mouth, maybe his tongue. He was certainly mobile, so I decided we'd hoof it for home. Hopefully, he'd be distracted by the run.

"Go, Kodiak," I said, urging him on to the Grass Dam. It was a winding snake across the ice.

"Go-go-go!"

Kodiak loves the lead sled dog game and started to trot across. I grabbed my gear and quickly followed. When we reached the opposite shore, we started running in the dark.

As soon as we shot through the door, Kodiak dropped the game and whined. I gasped for air, pulled off my foggy glasses, and snapped on the lights.

"Come here. I'll fix it," I said, hoping I wasn't lying. Quills are a problem. Kodes has been anaesthetized twice after porcupine encounters, and that was only after our first few experiences left him so traumatized that he was afraid of pliers for a week. I looked into his mouth.

What was this?

I was a bit disgusted, but mostly with myself. An imagination is a terrible thing to waste, especially on unfounded fears. I'd almost made it rationally out the other side. Almost.

"Here, hold still. I'll get it." Kodiak held still, and I reached in and extracted a three-inch length of tree root that was wedged across the roof of his mouth. It popped right out, and I held it up for Kodiak to inspect.

"This is your big problem?" I asked. "Have you been digging holes all this time?"

He sniffed the stick, then trotted over and began to eat his dog food. He was over it already.

I noticed I had sweat through my wool sweater, and my stomach hurt a little, but I was too tired to care, and it didn't matter anyway. There had been no real harm done, no phone calls to the electric company, at least, and we had had a great walk. I was on sabbatical to discover more about winter, but it seemed there were other lessons to be learned as well. I settled into the chair by the stove. Not a bad first day off.

Home for the Holiday

"Red barns, brown hay, white snow, the colors of a working ranch in winter."

Light rain in the early morning; typical. Whenever we're packing to go to Michigan for the holiday break, the weather keeps us guessing. Skis? Skates? Fly rods? There was that December afternoon at the Manistee below Tippy Dam trying to thaw my fingers, watching other anglers catch steelhead. Fortunately, David and our hometown friend Coh were there; camaraderie keeps me warm. Pack the presents; that's a given. We had already packed most of them, along with Kodiak's dog-dunnage. Clothes, the part we both dread, are packed last. Gear? Warm gloves and denim jackets that will shed hay are out there in our closet, waiting as if we'd never left. Rain coats? I hope not. It always seems to take a little effort to get winter started.

The rain looked odd by noon, trying to turn to snow. I set the rodmakers' list serv to postpone e-mail delivery, called the post office and had our regular mail re-routed to a neighbor, and tried to fool Kodiak into thinking that I wasn't packing. He gets to go, as always, but it's nice to postpone the dog-excitement until the last minute. He'd sit in the truck all night, ready, if he knew what was up.

Schools started letting out early as the weather changed, and David was home by three. We decided to drive the truck into town for some last minute presents since we'd be leaving just as soon as he could get home from work the next day. The rain had changed entirely to wet snow by the time we made our way back. All of our world seemed hushed again. Once inside, we added the presents and some clothes to the mound to be loaded into the truck. Kodiak would ride up front with us on his bed between our air bags, and we'd have four wheel drive, our best guess to handle a week's worth of changing conditions.

There are a lot of nice sounds to go to sleep by: the water's babble from a lean-to on Roaring Brook in Baxter State Park, the crackle of the fire in the woodstove, the low rumble of a Michigan thunderstorm, or the sound of David's laughter and talk with Coh drifting up from downstairs, planning for our arrival. In the loft, I could just catch occasional words: bamboo, plowed roads, capitalism, faceless institutions, good beer. More laughter. That's how those conversations go. The sound of friends.

Two days later, we were just into Michigan. By one a.m., Janet called it a night, and Kodiak and I curled up on the couch, waiting for Coh and David to come back from Coh's shop. Coh wholesales rod blanks and associated good stuff, talking fishing all day with anglers and rodmakers or builders from all over. Not a bad way to live. I need a clone on nights like those; I want to be in the shop, and I want to catch up with Janet. Coh promised they'd be back early and go down to the shop again with me in the morning, but I know how that goes. The best talk is at night, even if it isn't actually as profound as it seems at the time.

David and I were a little road weary, anyway. The wet snow had persisted through the Thursday night phone conversation with Coh into Friday morning. David let Kodiak out at five a.m., and I turned on the TV. The unfortunate part of snow days is that it takes longer to drive into town in bad weather, so waiting to hear the school closings is a bit of a gamble. If we wait too long and school isn't closed, we'll be late; if we leave with time to drive through the snow, we won't know if school is canceled until we're well into the storm. David had the truck running, and I was trying to focus on the tiny lines at the bottom of the screen when the phone rang. No school. I could live with that.

We napped until the storm waned at eight a.m., and then suited up. David ran the snowblower, a struggle in a foot of wet snow, and I cleared off the vehicles and alternated them out of his way. While he opened the driveway, I re-shoveled the decks, covered again since his five o'clock effort, and then shoveled the backdoor landing as far as the birdfeeders. I switched from throwing the heavy snow with the shovel to moving it with the scoop, a giant shovel with molded runners and an inverted U-shaped handle, great for leaning into at my waist and applying some real power. I pushed each shovelful over the bank, running as I scooped up each load to gain enough momentum to climb it. I had just reached my best speed when the scoop hit something and stopped dead, the handle nearly knocking the wind out of me.

I looked up to see David watching, my usual luck, but he was having his own problems. The snow was getting heavier with the rising temperatures, and he could barely blow it. He'd just broken a sheer pin and was nearly out of gas. Time for lunch.

After snowshoeing to the north drive to scoop out the banks left by the plow and checking the canoe shed roof, I retreated to pack the truck. Kodiak couldn't be duped any longer and jumped in to wait for the Big Ride. He was still there at four when David put the snowblower away. It was a late start, but the stars came out by five, and the roads were clear. We were on our way to Michigan.

There are few sights so engaging as New England at Christmastime: white clapboard houses decorated with garlands of balsam fir, icicles and icicle lights outlining the eves; barns roofed with fresh snow lit by moonlight, warm windows revealing sheep, cattle, and horses inside. Every small town has a tree decorated in the square. We followed the Androscoggin River into New Hampshire listening to the Paul Winter solstice concert on public radio. Solstice, the shortest day, winter.

The evening was effortless and beautiful. Kodiak slept between us with his head on my lap. I thought it wouldn't be so bad to just have the moment go on forever. Unfortunately, traveling with Kodiak, it nearly did. It wasn't until the far side of Vermont that we found a place to sleep that accepted dogs. David moved us in for the night while I walked Kodiak, discretely far from the lodge so the owners wouldn't find anything to make them change their minds in the future. Even with the late start, we had shaved enough miles off the trip to leave time for bad weather and/or some time to visit Janet and Coh.

We crossed Lake Champlain before breakfast in the morning, topped out with Mohawk gas at Akwesasne, and crossed into Canada by eight. I read *The Fellowship of the Ring* aloud to jog old memories before the new movie. Coh, David, and I had made a pilgrimage of sorts to Wales in college, backpacking from train to train on the little cash we three could scrape together. In Cardiff, Coh's supposed ancestral home, we learned that J.R.R. Tolkien was buried near Oxford, where he taught. We each bought a gold plastic ring, symbolic of the evil ring from his stories and of our economic status, and sought out the English university. They gave us directions to the cemetery where we borrowed a small triple-forked branch from some shrubbery and left the three rings on its fingers at Tolkein's grave.

At Port Huron customs, the border patrol was out in large numbers but the crossing was quick. In a couple of hours, while David and Coh picked up pizza for supper, Janet, Ashley, Kelsey, and I were playing "Go Fly Fish," a card game like Fish but with flies and their histories that the girls had given their dad.

We didn't go back down to the shop in the morning, as suspected. I'd lost the urge, anyway. Then it started snowing on our way north, but it was like a first snow of the year, exciting and harmless. Our spirits were high. Home. There really is no place like it. We made the ritual stop at Jay's Sporting Goods when we left the freeway, and then it was just the last leg to our home town. It was great to cruise Main Street again. The last time we were home, we were talking bamboo at the library. Lilas, the librarian, had made cookies for the event, and we stayed five hours. It felt like old friends, and was.

Dorothy and Barb had arrived home a few days before us; David's mother had flown to Maine to keep his sister company on the long drive to Michigan, making Barb home early enough to help prepare for the holidays. Kodiak was rubber-legged to find them and the fenced in back yard where he could bark hello to the neighbor's chocolate lab.

Then, at last, the farm where I grew up. We have a house and barns that once belonged to my parents. When Darius Scott came from England, he homesteaded in Ohio and then followed the frontier north in a covered wagon when his son Bert moved to Michigan. Bert and Louisa cleared land and raised their crops, cattle, and children, one son being my grandfather, Myrl. Grandpa married a little French girl named Lettie, and they herded cattle ahead of them to a section of land they split with Swedish farmers. As my father and his sisters were born, my grandparents added rooms around the original two that made the farmhouse, hosted a barn-raising, and eventually switched from horses to tractors.

Dad and Mom added new land to the farm, and I began my formal education in the same one-room school he attended, my older brother and I playing in the haymow when we weren't doing chores. But time caught up with us all. Mom went to work in town as the family farm lost its place in history, and my little sister and brother started school there, too. Dad took over the entire farm and converted it to a ranching operation as crop prices and the deer herd added their impact to the uncertainty of growing conditions and the intensity needed for a lucrative dairy operation. Eventually, I was lucky enough to gain stepparents I truly love, and David and I bought the house my parents built to replace the old farmhouse.

Still, life is full of irony. After years of working in and around hay, I finally developed hay fever, allergies so severe that I was reduced to tractor driving each June when everyone else could help in the mows. I delivered a load of hay, went in to wash my face, and cried until the wagon was empty when I realized my fate. Then I went back out and drove to the field for another load.

When we walked into our house, the phone was ringing. Dad must have ESP. I looked out the window to the west; the other side of the farm is beyond the trees, beyond the lake, but I felt like he was close enough to touch. His voice was welcoming, casual, but something was hidden there.

"What have you been up to?" he asked. I laughed. What had I been up to? Driving home. A good joke. I told him about the trip out.

"What have you been up to?" I asked him.

"Not much. Chores." There was a pause. " My heart rate has been a little slow, about thirty this morning. Just a second, I'm taking it right now."

Thirty seemed just a bit slow to me.

"Hmm," his voice was saying, "it's only twenty-eight. That can't be right."

He wasn't interested in the emergency room, even when my stepmother Sue joined him on the line, and we lamely tried to disguise it as a dinner outing. They invited us to dinner instead. On the bright side, we wouldn't have to be unpacking that night.

Dad was himself, and supper was great. We all moved into the living room to watch something on satellite TV. From Dad's command center in his recliner, he's in sight of both the computer in the spare room and the window of the bedroom in the little empty house next door where he was born one December. Grandma really did put him in the wood cookstove to keep him warm. Earlier that day, she'd split the kindling for it herself. Grandma always had cookies for us, frozen chocolate chip cookies in her freezer in the summer that we'd grab between loads of hay. Thinking of her made my heart ache for Dad, but he was busy being analytical, and the memory passed.

During commercials, Dad was answering questions about his medications. Was he taking something that might slow him down and needed readjusting? That was my hope, the best-case scenario. Sue was saying something, and Dad paused. Literally paused.

Then he gripped the chair a little tighter and said sheepishly, "Whew, everything just shut down for a minute." He grinned. David and I looked at each other.

When we called the next morning, Dad announced that he'd lived through the night. He had a doctor's appointment for 9:45, after he fed the cattle. We offered to ride along, if that was okay, to climb off and on the tractor, opening gates and pulling the strings off bales. He said it was okay.

Of all the ranchwork, feeding the cattle in the winter is my favorite. I'd looked forward to it all of the way home: the warm tractor; the snow on the cows' shaggy backs; the yearling calves frisking in the hay; the deliberate, stately bulls, handsome and potentially dangerous. Crisp air, big lake-effect snowflakes, cattle munching. All's right with the world.

The tractors and even the bales have evolved over the years, but it was still basically the same, except that, this year, on Christmas Eve, there was a secret. We all knew it; we said nothing. But when Dad set the new, four-wheel drive tractor into motion, we watched everything he did. When he lifted a five-foot high round bale from the big open barn with the prong on the front loader, we watched and learned. Which barn, which hay, which controls, which gears. David and I have always hung out with Dad on the farm, helping whenever there was opportunity. We always asked questions, but this time the answers carried a bit more explanation, and we memorized every move. Just in case. Then we rode back up to the house with him, and retrieved the bareback saddle he and Sue had picked up for us to give to a niece. It was forest green wool, and she could add stirrups later. Dad hurried to get ready, and they were off to the doctor's.

While we were wrapping presents for that evening's Christmas Eve celebration with David's family, we waited. Most of the gifts had decorative bags designated for them before we left Maine. If Canadian border customs had really cracked down, we would have been glad they were easy to inspect. As it turned out, we had sailed through unsearched. You never know. I matched gifts with tags and disguised the contents of the bags with tissue paper while David wrapped the saddle. Then Sue called to say they were admitting Dad until they could implant a pacemaker. My grandfather had had the first pacemaker in the township. For my family and our neighbors, he was the first person we ever knew with one, and it made a lasting impression. It was during those years when time noticed we'd been by-passed, and things were changing quickly. David and I weren't really surprised at the news. We made a list of things Dad needed from home and headed to the hospital. This was it; the secret was out.

Christmas Eve dinner was wonderful. Dad had been so okay, more than okay, lying there in blue jeans in his hospital bed, that there was no reason to suspect he wouldn't be fine. He had fed his herd with a heart rate of thirty for two days. We had made it back to the farm with time to walk Kodiak back behind the barn and smile at the beauty of the brown tips of birdsfoot trefoil, clover, alfalfa, and the grasses rising just above the bright snow before driving to town.

Dorothy had us all together, her family: daughter Barb, then son David and I on her left, older son Bill then Gloria to her right, beside the granddaughters, Barbie and then Kariann and her fiancée Carlos, already one of us. We feasted, talked, and laughed, but mostly just cared for each other with renewed appreciation. Almost every dish was washed before the service at Dorothy's

Lutheran Church, where afterwards we enjoyed quick visits with childhood friends. Our tradition of a family snapshot carried us into presents, and the saddle Barbie wanted, and finally the box of mixed chocolates. Then together we lingered, relaxed.

We started sampling desserts again and focused on Kariann and Carlos. He'd been telling us about his most embarrassing moment at dinner, and we all knew an opportunity to add another one to his list when we saw it. Maybe, if you are only twenty and you were raised in the city downstate, you have reason to believe there will be a gas station open in our small town on Christmas Eve. Carlos announced that he didn't have enough gas to drive to the farm that evening, let alone downstate on Christmas morning, and, in all fairness, we took pity and shooed them off to look for an open station just before ten.

When they limped back, Carlos offered an excuse, and we couldn't resist.

"It's not my fault."

"It's your trailblazer."

"But I wasn't driving."

"You know," we cautioned him, "we're not sure that watching a DVD in the back seat while Kariann drives is an excuse you should use." She agreed.

We went on for a while, offering bad ideas, not offering ideas, or generally being no help at all, until everyone was laughing and we gave in. I dug out the phone book and offered numbers of stations within a reasonable radius until we found one open. By two a.m., David and I were back home with my family's presents bagged for Christmas Day, and we had a few hours to sleep.

David and I were a little giddy mounting the steps to the cab of the big blue tractor Christmas morning. Dad has always had

Fords, now New Hollands, and they're always kept immaculately clean. David took the seat, and I sat on the lid of the toolbox, a comfy perch usually occupied by the barn cat. The two of us fit with room to spare. We looked over the controls, mostly familiar from the day before. We were ready. Where was the key? We both laughed. Probably something I should have asked. Then I remembered where Dad had always kept his keys, and the big diesel roared to life.

We experimented with the controls while the tractor warmed up. Old front loaders were usually just scoops which could carry and dump a load. This one worked more like a robot arm. Extending from the middle of the loader's crossbar was a three-foot long spike, three inches in diameter and pointed at the end. This could be slipped into the end of one of the big round bales just above center then rocked upwards to carry the bale securely. A minor spike on either side would keep the bale from twisting.

On the rear of the tractor another device for transporting big round bales looked like two opposing arms that could be swung open hydraulically. At the end of the arms were cones that center into the ends of the bale when the arms are closed to embrace it. The bale can be lifted for transport or lowered to roll it out on the ground for the cattle. Round bales aren't actually round, but are rolls of hay like huge Swiss roll cakes.

We backed out.

The biggest hay barn is just across the road, on the same side as the original farm buildings. Red barns, brown hay, white snow. The colors of a working ranch in winter. David manipulated a bale from the top row and backed out to set it near the gate. He drove back in and speared a second, from the row below, and backed up again, this time securing the first bale in the arms on the back of the tractor. He lifted it, and we headed for the pasture with both.

Thirty-three cows, as many calves, and a single bull, all of them shaggy with snow covered backs, lifted their heads to check us out. Same tractor, same time, same hay, different people. I climbed down to handle the big orange metal gate, and David drove through. While I secured the gate again, he lowered the bale to within my reach. It was snowing big, beautiful flakes, Michigan style. With lake effect snow and any breeze, the flakes travel parallel to the ground. There were only a couple of inches of accumulation, except where the travel had been interrupted and the flakes had collapsed into a drift.

I slipped off my mitten, pulled out my jackknife, and looked for the orange nylon twine wound around the bale in a spiral. Each time I found a round of twine imbedded in the hay, I cut it and wound the loose end around my mittened hand. When I'd cut them all, I pocketed the knife and pulled the right mitten back on. Then I pulled all of the twine off the first bale at once and wound up the string. The cows all watched.

David lifted the bale higher and moved forward to drop it into the circular metal feeder, a hoop target in a sea of shuffling cattle. The cows closed in to eat, and he backed up to me again. I removed the twine from the rear bale and climbed into the warm cab. We lowered the bale to touch the ground and moved ahead, letting it unroll. A wide swath of hay trailed behind us across the snow, and the young cattle romped in it as if the season had suddenly turned to spring. Just as I had hoped, just as it should be.

We retrieved two more bales and headed south toward the lake and a pasture far from the road.

The cattle were divided into two herds. The ones we fed first were just across from the bale barn in a pasture adjacent to the corrals and small barns. The second half of the cattle were in their fall pasture nearly a half-mile away. It's a place of rolling hills, birch and oak for shelter, and small alder wetlands decorated with winterberry, Michigan holly. The lake lies just beyond the reach of the cattle through the wetlands but joins with the hills of the summer pasture beyond. These cattle are more range habituated than the ones by the road. They rarely see any sign of other humans until winter. They knew that the tractor meant good hay, though, and they came over to investigate when I climbed down to open the gate.

"Hi, there," I said, stepping off the tractor into ankle deep snow. "Remember me from yesterday?"

The cows kept their distance, but at least they didn't run. I moved slowly, cattle speed, making a quick scan for the two bulls, still apparently over the hill. The gate was an older four-post, four strands of barbed wire type, looking like an elaborate tic tac toe game. We'd had these all my life, and I knew how to take the stick wired to the gate post, lever the gate toward me so I could slip its retaining loop up over the post, then lift the first upright out of the bottom loop, and swing the gate back wide against the fence so no errant calf would step in it and tangle itself.

David waited for me to proceed; Dad had said that the cattle would follow the tractor so we could leave the gate open while we worked, but it seemed risky to me. I hurried over, stepping into a snow-disguised hole, and tumbled down into the fresh powder. I came up quickly, white and laughing. The cows retreated over the hill, too weird for them. Obviously, the gate would be fine. We drove to the sheltered bowl in the hills where Dad had fed them.

The cattle were excited to see the hay coming. Their hunger overshadowed any anxiety they'd had about me, and they crowded around the tractor when David stopped to let me out.

"Want me to help?" he asked, as I dismounted into a sea of cattle.

I was pretty sure I'd be okay. "Nah, but keep the door open," I grinned.

Dad's cattle are not mean. In fact, with their winter coats they had curly foreheads and looked cuddly. They were already stealing any bits of hay they could free from the two bales, though, and could get so preoccupied with eating that they'd forget there was a hundred pound human in their midst. Even the calves outweighed me by a few hundred pounds, and an ill-placed frolic could mean trouble. Best to keep them all well aware of my presence now that they'd decided not to be afraid. Banter had always worked well, so I was glad to be in a back pasture. David couldn't even hear me over the purr of the diesel.

"Hey, cows," I said, "this is my hay. Why don't you just move back a bit while I cut these strings? I'll just cut these hard to find strings here, and pull them off, and then you can have this whole bale."

I described every move I was making to them. The strings, of course, were stuck, frozen to the bale. I had to pull them off one at a time.

"Just a minute, cows. I'm having a little trouble here. You'll get your hay if you'll just be patient." I looked up from the bale to find two cows tentatively reaching in from either side of me, both with nose extended, pink muscular tongue reaching out.

"Not now!" I stamped one foot. They both retreated. "I said 'in a minute'!"

Two more moved in while I wrestled the next string.

"Hey!" I yelled. "There seems to be some confusion here. This is MY HAY! I am the titan and you must wait!"

I was laughing and struggling with the frozen strings. Man! I sure hoped no one could hear this. I went on, though.

"You are the cows," I put one foot on the middle of the bale, " and you eat when the pitiful weakling says so." I wrapped the last strings around my mitten and heaved back as two more moved in on my right and left.

"You are the COWS!" I groaned and pulled the strings free. I started winding them with the others on my hand when I noticed the company I was keeping.

"Oops," I apologized, "you are not the cows." The two bulls, each eight feet long and two thousand pounds, were standing on either side of me, content to munch my hay. Their hay, as far as I was concerned. All either one had to do was swing his rear toward the other, and I'd be trapped. Maybe I could get up over the bale. I looked up; probably not. Years ago, a bull had been sampling a bale Dad was unstringing, tossed his head, and innocently sent Dad flying through the air. Dad had told me, with broken ribs, how it was just an accident.

Both of these bulls had a mouthful and were standing still, so I chanced slipping out the chute between them and then made a grand circle around the herd to the front of the tractor. David, who had been hidden the whole time by the hay, finally came into view as I crossed toward the open door. Doomed never to make a graceful entrance, I immediately caught my toe on a frozen cowpie and was down again. I was up fast, but I was laughing so hard I could barely climb into the cab.

The bale rolled out beautifully, and the gentle cattle moved in. The calves pranced about, and the snow had started falling again in those big lazy flakes by the time we lowered the front bale and removed its strings together. They came off easily. We lingered to watch the cattle grazing the swath of hay from the first bale, to listen to them, to watch the snow fall around them. The hills rose up white to shelter their valley, and there was peace everywhere we looked. The second bale rolled out smoothly, and I strung the gate again after we passed through.

Sue had talked to Dad while we were working. The night nurses had moved him into intensive care ("Someone got nervous," he said), but the day nurses had moved him back to his room. Sue had finished feeding the horses, seventeen Tennessee Walkers which share the barns, stalls, and riding arenas nearest the house, and she was ready to go to my sister's house for our family Christmas. She'd stay a bit, then head to the hospital. It was also Dad and Sue's anniversary. They had been married with David and me as attendants, grandchildren at their feet, years ago in front of the Christmas tree.

Karla and Richard have opened their home nestled in the woods to our ever-extending family for Christmas for years. Nieces Holly and Sarah met us in the yard and helped carry in food and presents, the first of the great flood. By noon, there were babies everywhere, four of them under two years old, nieces and nephews chattering, my aunt, my cousin, and various visitors by telephone until the food was prepared, and Karla called for quiet. It was almost a Christmas miracle to hear the sudden hush in the room. My cousin Steve, the most reverent of our group, began speaking, and I heard his prayer change to words about Dad. I had to shut my eyes to hold back tears. It almost worked. There's something about the support of a close family that makes it okay to take a minute off.

Mid-afternoon, after our second feast of the holiday, after pictures and presents, and conversations over dishes, and hugs good-bye, we were among the last to leave. Karla and Rich would be at the hospital with Dad and Sue for awhile, so we went home to walk Kodiak, a good, long walk, and then check on the assorted livestock before driving to the hospital ourselves. We stayed watching old John Wayne movies with Dad until visiting hours were over.

We fed the cattle by the road as the sun was coming up and drove through big flakes of slowly blowing horizontal snow back to the ranged half of the herd. The bulls were totally preoccupied with a dominance issue, and the strings on the bales came off quickly. We had unrolled the first bale and were unrolling the second when a fight broke out. Bullfights are slow, deliberate shows of power, and usually less like actual fighting than leaning into one another. They don't run to butt heads; they slowly press their foreheads together and push with two thousand pounds of weight and muscle. As long as the bulls are the same size, no one wins and no harm is done, unless one bull makes a mistake.

We watched as the rest of the cattle continued grazing the swath, and the bulls slowly moved away. Then one slipped, started to fall and caught himself, and fell victim to a slow motion push back toward the hay. When they were directly over it, in line with the cows, the bulls suddenly smelled hay below their lowered, butted heads, and stopped to eat. Fight over.

"Wow," we both whispered. We have real respect for that power. As we put the tractor away, we shook our heads over the way the two bulls had just forgotten the whole fight when they noticed the hay.

David had showered, and I was almost done when the well pump quit working. Was it the pump or the well? David couldn't answer because the phone rang; Sue called to say they'd moved Dad's surgery up three hours. We found the snow intensifying when we went out to the well pit and realized we didn't know when they'd take Dad from the room or how long the drive would take in the ill-timed storm. We decided to leave a quick message on the wellman's answering machine. He was just a guy who'd helped us with the well three years before when the screen had plugged, admittedly a long shot. We threw the breaker off and left.

Dad was in a great humor, although his veins weren't cooperating with the nurse, and his IV could have worked better. Still, he likes learning new things. We were barely there a half-hour before we all rode down the elevator together with the team in blue scrubs. The back door of the elevator opened to go to surgery; I remembered that from when I was six years old and had had my tonsils out. Dad was chatting with the team when they took him down the last hallway, and we went with Sue to wait.

I had wondered how long the time would seem. They say that pacemaker surgery is fairly routine, but I couldn't tell if I believed it or not, even though I knew it was true. Another one of those heart versus head battles.

There was no doubt that people were watching over us. A neighbor in scrubs was with Dad. Another peeked out from behind a desk to motion Sue over because a third was feeding her horses right then and was on the phone for more details. We made our way to the cafeteria where still another neighbor arrived, one who had gone to school with Dad, farmed nearby, and had hired me to baby-sit during my teens. He had stopped up to see Dad, not knowing the surgery had been moved up, and to offer to do what he could to help with the farm during any recovery time. There are moments when I suddenly realize I'm home, like suddenly realizing it's Christmas.

Dad was chatting with the team in blue on his way back up the hallway to us and all of the way up in the elevator. They'd only needed a local anesthetic, he remembered nothing, and his heart was pumping at a steady sixty beats per minute, the fastest rhythm it had maintained, apparently, for a long time. My brother Alan called from North Carolina to wish him luck with the surgery but had the distinction of being the first call back in the room instead. David and I slipped out while the nurses finished reattaching the monitors and ran into my aunt and cousin who'd come for support but joined the party instead. Dad was sitting up on the side of the bed eating supper when we went home to call the neighbors. We arrived to find our driveway plowed and truck tracks leading to our well.

We fed the cattle the next morning, Thursday, while Sue drove up to bring Dad home. We walked Kodiak all around the farm while we waited, then joined them at the ranchhouse to make sure everything was okay. The evening we spent with David's mom and family. Two days to go. We still hadn't unpacked.

Friday morning, we had just retrieved the first two bales from the barn when Dad arrived. It was good to see his white pickup parked next to ours. David gave him the tractor seat and moved to the toolbox. I ducked down again between Dad's knee and the door. It was Monday morning all over again. We talked just a little about pacemakers (his was computerized to kick out if his heart raced over sixty), about Grandpa, about the past week, but the calves still had to be weaned, and the ranged half of the herd needed to be moved closer. The past faded into its proper place, and we finalized plans for the round up the next morning. As soon as the cattle were fed, we traded the big spike for the actual loader bucket, then piled in fencing tools and spent the rest of the afternoon securing the winter pastures.

We walked that evening along the shores of the Doc and Tom, a tributary of the Muskegon River, with Karla. The stream is only inches deep with a sandy bottom, but it was hidden by a snowy blanket and made a white ribbon beneath the trees. We're long distance sisters, living different lives in different worlds, not always easy. Winter walks together in beautiful places are precious. Then we went inside to find Rich and make plans for the work coming up in the morning.

There's always a little prep work before any major activity. We met Dad early and went up to the big, red, gambrel-roofed barn my grandparents had raised. The young cattle would winter there, sheltered where Dad could feed them grain and the highest quality hay while he watched stock prices, the real stock market. David and I went upstairs to throw hay and straw from the mows through the holes built into the floor above the mangers and open pens below. Then we spread the golden straw for bedding, spread the hay the length of the mangers. The calves would be shut in for a few days until they lost the urge to find their way back to the herd down the road. Then they would be free to come and go, using the bottom of the big barn for shelter and food, roaming the pasture down as far as the bale barn. Dad kept his left arm lower than his shoulder, as per the doctor's order. I held my breath in the sparkling chaff when I could and stepped outside for fresh air when my allergies were too much.

At nine, Rich and Sue joined us at the corrals. We opened two back gates, and the close half of the herd came right through, as the cows had every year of their lives, into the small holding pasture. From there, we walked slowly behind them, fanning out to form a barrier but never moving too quickly. The herd moved slowly into the first corral. It was a tight fit with the cows, their calves, a bull, and the five of us, but we kept our actions subtle, trying not to get anyone too excited, bovine or human.

Each of us carried a long herding stick, an extension of our arms that would persuade a slightly nervous calf which way to go with a mere wave of the wand. Dad manned the gate. The trick was to let the cows and bull back out into the holding field, and eventually back into their pasture, but keep the calves in the corral. The calves, of course, were quick, but the cows had done it before, and, being creatures of habit, were more or less cooperative. Some of the wilder calves bolted into the adjacent corral, which was their next destination anyway, so we closed them in, let the last few cows out, and had the herd sorted in no time.

The calves had a little time to calm down while Dad went to get the stock trailer. We walked to that barn to help him hook it to the tractor. The stock trailer looks like a longer, lower horse trailer, and can haul a dozen calves at a time. Being grazers by nature, calves aren't eager to go in through the dark doorway into a denlike trailer, but it's an easy, low step up and there are humane ways to persuade them.

Dad backed the stock trailer up to the chute at the end of the last corral, and we slid open the rear door. It was time to see just how cooperative the calves were going to be. Sue and I used our usual strategy; we kept totally out of sight, hiding behind the low barn that makes up one side of the corrals. I had hand painted that barn once to earn money for college. Dad, Rich, and David gently urged the calves through the series of corrals. Each time they passed through a gate, the next corral was smaller. The gate behind them would swing to scoot the calves along provided they felt agreeable. It's hard to scoot thirty-three, five hundred-pound calves if they're feeling defiant or nervous, so Sue and I kept hidden. No sense adding to the distractions; three in the pen was already a crowd.

The first few calves headed up the long, narrow, board-sided chute to the stock trailer with no problem. When they reached the dark entrance, they stopped. Dad gently prodded the back calves, hoping for a little chain reaction peer pressure, but the first calf had sized up the situation and decided to try to turn around and retreat. We all stepped forward and urged the other calves the length of the chute to change his mind, and the next six pushed him inside. The halfway gate was swung shut, and five more went in peacefully. We slid the back door shut.

Rich rode up to the big barn to help unload the calves, but Sue, David, and I stayed behind. The sun had finally come out; it had been gray all week. Unloading the calves is pretty easy: back up to the barn, open the door and gate, and off they go. We talked and admired the remaining calves until all was calm, then separated them into two trailer-sized groups. Dad and Rich returned, and we loaded eleven, then, later, ten. All thirty-three calves were in the big barn, and the cows and bull were back in their winter pasture. Dad felt good; we all felt good. It was time to bring up the wilder, ranged half of the herd.

We spread some hay in the first holding pen and opened its gate to the road. Dad and Rich picked up a bale of hay on the rear of the tractor to use as bait of a sort and headed through the open gate directly across the road to the back pasture to get the cattle. Sue, David, and I spread the hay out, sprinkling a little on the deserted morning road so the first cows would see it as they approached. Then we split up to position vehicles on down the road to the east and west, a warning to cars and a deterrent to wandering cattle. We turned on our flashers and waited. It was nice to be in the warm pickup. It was snowing and blowing again.

The cattle came on a dead run. They were ahead of the tractor, racing for the gates. They didn't pause on the road but crossed straight through to the spread hay, mooing and snorting. The calves kicked up their heels; the cows had done this before, but it was new territory to their offspring. Dad and Rich brought up the rear and took their bale on into the first corral as we closed the road gate. The cattle followed the bale, pushing and shoving, until Dad dropped it in the corral and brought the tractor back out. This was an enthusiastic herd. Maybe a bit too lively.

The five of us regrouped, watching them. Dad half decided to leave the calves in the corral for a few days, once they were separated. This barn could be opened for shelter, and they would be near their mothers in the adjacent field. These calves would have some time to calm down, and so would the first group, already up in the big barn, before they were herded together.

"That is," Dad said, "providing they don't just break the corral down."

As before, it was a very tight fit in the corral with a big bale of hay, fifty cows, fifty calves, the two bulls, and the five of us. We were all on heightened alert as Dad stepped over to man the gate again. Sue stood as the last defense before him, and I was just south of them both. David and Rich were between Sue and me in an arc, so that we would get the calves to go to the back of the square corral where I'd cut them off, and the guys would redirect the cows toward Sue. She'd make sure no calves slipped by toward Dad, who would swing the gate open a crack to let cows, only, out.

There was a lot of potential energy in our midst; we would be trying to divide an excitable herd.

A few cows had the idea right off, and I had a few cornered calves staring at me, front legs spread and heads low, trying to decide whether to bolt. David and Richard were next, handling the bulk of the herd, when I heard Dad yelling over to Sue that a calf was getting by. I looked up to see that Sue was looking the other way, past Rich. Just behind him, the bulls had started fighting.

"The bulls are fighting!" I called to Dad. "Rich, the bulls are behind you!"

David and Rich stepped away from the slow motion power show just as one huge bull turned sideways and a ton of adversary pushed him broadside. They slammed into the side of the corral and one went down, rolled in slow motion by his own great weight and the steam engine which wouldn't quit. Four strands of barbed wire, the corral top board, and a tall wooden fencepost couldn't hold them back.

We opened the gate into the holding pen and the cows and calves streamed out. Dad chased the victor out behind them, and the victim stood complaining and trying to kick a loop of woven wire fence off his rear foot. I thought he was being remarkably sensible about it. The five of us stood blocking the gaping hole in the corral as the victim freed his foot and bellowed off, and the victor answered from the other side of the fence. There were some major ill feelings there all right. Two cows left in the corral with us went on munching hay. No business of theirs.

"Bet that pacemaker kicked off that time, " I grinned. Whether or not Dad's heart rate had pushed itself above the pacemaker's sixty beat maximum, mine might have gone a bit higher.

The sun came out with the gear to fix the fence, which we rebuilt while the poor fellow complained around the adjacent pasture. I wondered if he might go hoarse. Dad and David untangled the strands of woven wire and matched them. Rich stepped into the pasture with the slowly deflating bull to lean the post back up. Good thing the ground still hadn't frozen hard; otherwise the post would have broken off.

Dad, on the tractor, took some hay out to calm the lone bull, and we decided to let him have the two remaining cows for company. They'd eventually end up in that pasture anyway. While Dad put the tractor away, the other four of us herded all of the calves and some of the cows, but definitely not the victorious bull, back into the corrals. Rich manned the gate, David cut the cows, and Sue and I directed calves.

Every cow was back in the holding pen before Dad walked back from putting the tractor away. He surveyed the situation: the bull and two cows were in the winter pasture already, the other bull and the rest of the cows were grazing on the hay we'd spread on the ground to get them to cross the road into the holding pen, and the calves were sandwiched in between. It was two o'clock.

"I think I'll leave them all where they are for now," he said, "and come back down later to let the rest of these into the pasture after they've cleaned up this hay." He and Rich would haul the calves to the big barn in a few days.

So we were done. It felt odd to have it suddenly over. Dad assured us that he felt fine, and there was nothing else to do right then. He and Sue offered to take us all out for lunch/ dinner, but it had finally hit us. We'd better re-group and see what to do. Rich went to town, and we left with a promise that we'd be back in the evening.

So there. Saturday midafternoon, and we'd be leaving on Sunday. What would we like to do? We went back to the house where Kodiak was waiting. What was the one thing we'd really like to do with our free afternoon? We decided that I'd take Kodiak off for his romp but carry a two-way radio, and David would call Wes Cooper. Wes is a well-respected bamboo rodmaker and has been a friendly source of advice on rod repair. He lives south of the farm seventy-five miles, over in the snowbelt, and we had promised we'd be back over for another visit. With any luck, he'd be home.

David radioed when I was coming back up the long hill behind the barn. Wes had injured his knee slipping on the ice and had spent two sleepless nights. His wife said he was finally getting some rest, and we didn't have the heart to wake him.

Free again. We didn't have to pack; we hadn't unpacked. I deliberately hadn't brought the fishing gear along. Two Decembers ago, Coh had been spending some time on the big part of the Manistee River where the steelhead congregate below Tippy Dam, and he'd enthusiastically offered to show us the ropes. He's our friend, and we were game, although I was in it more for the chance to spend the day on the river than having any hope of connecting with big fish. David and I generally alternate our fishing when Kodiak is around, and that was fine with me for steelheading, too. If David caught something, I'd give it a try. Otherwise, I was going for the reconnaissance.

No one was at the river when we arrived. We all layered in warm clothes, grabbed armloads of gear and refreshments (I had hot chocolate, believing that any cold beverage in December on the river is just further proof of insanity), and started down the long staircase to the water. The Manistee has high sand banks, and the steps prevent erosion plus they would give me a chance to warm up by running up and down them every time someone discovered something we'd forgotten in the car. Coh was in his element and cheerfully rigged up and waded in. David and I watched him for awhile; then David followed suit. They cast big rods with heavy lines and mammoth flies, and I watched with curiosity. Just when I'd decided that the scenery was the best part, a steelhead surfaced like a great white shark. It laughed at my fishing companions and went under to await the arrival of a different species of angler, the steelhead drill team.

They arrived just at three, after we'd been fishing for six hours with no luck, I'd thawed my fingers in the car twice, an eagle had flown over, and we'd laughed over enough good stories to make up for the months we'd be apart until summer. These guys had done this before. They headed directly for the river's edge below us, fanning out to leave just enough space to cast a spinning rod without impaling the next guy on their hooks. Egg sacks were flying through the air, and, one, two, three, flashing steelhead were fighting their captors and charging upstream. Lines were pulled out of the way, the steelhead met their fates, and the anglers retreated as quickly as they had arrived. One hour, they were gone. We had the river to ourselves again.

I decided that I'd stick to the upper Manistee. I love dry fly fishing in the Deward tract in summer, camping out in the evening to the sound of nighthawks and coyotes. Or in April, nymphing a little farther down, just below the military base where the shores are deserted, and Kodiak can run free. Smaller rods, more delicate flies, wilder places. A river with something for everyone.

The hours of our last afternoon on the farm dwindled. We called Janet and Coh to finalize arrangements for the morning. We'd caravan with Barb and Dorothy and detour that way after breakfast on our trip back east. Or, if Dad would accept some help with chores, it would be more like noon. Probably we'd be early; he'd only missed three mornings, and he thought it would have been only two if they'd put pacemakers in on Christmas Day.

Sue served freshly baked bread with supper, and we stayed through the evening. Dad was all set for morning, so this would be good-bye until summer. We have a close telephone relationship, but it's not the same. We left reluctantly, but we had to finish winterizing the house and wrap those last few presents, the ones for Janet and Coh and the kids.

By ten that night, we were finished. Kodiak had gone off to bed as soon as David finished vacuuming and the house was quiet. David was next; he'd be driving at seven and then for two days. I turned off the lights and sat in the window for awhile, looking over the farm.

The sky was finally clear, and the moon was full and high. It reflected off the snow and illuminated the world where I grew up. They say you can never go home again, but what if you've never really left? I could see the lone elm tree standing in the blue-white pasture south of the house, the tops of the grasses still reaching above the snow in the hayfields, the deep red color of the moonlit barn. Magical, or am I just one of Tolkein's hobbits, in love with the Shire? I watched the stillness for a long time and wondered about the uncertain future of the farm and my love for our ponds in Maine, grateful for a good life full of good places and good people. I made a mental note to write Ward across the road a thank you for plowing the driveway. The tracks looked like his. Then I joined David and Kodiak for a little rest before our trip in the morning.

MID WINTER

––––––––

Nature says,

"I'm going to snow.

If you have on a bikini

and no snowshoes,

that's tough.

I am going to snow

anyway."

Maya Angelou

Ice Skating
New Year's Day

"There's something very
ravenlike about gliding across
a boreal pond in winter."

Like finding change in the pocket of your winter coat when you dig it out of the closet in November, returning home to Maine to find it hadn't snowed in more than a week was an unexpected and welcomed treat. Rather than spend the first day of the new year digging out, we were surprisingly free. Sure, there's always something that has to be done, especially with a rodmaker in the house, but freebies aren't to be squandered. We took our day as a gift to be treated as seriously as was appropriate. We'd go ice skating.

We had to decide where to go. Skating on wild ice has a lot of positive attributes: exercise, the freedom of fluid motion, the exhilaration of speed, the raw opportunity to improve balance in the face of the unexpected obstacle. It's also a good chance to travel unimpeded. Long distances on big lakes can be covered quickly, with complementary views to hiking along the shore but a lot more of them in the same amount of time. The perspective of looking from the water toward the shore is the same as when canoeing but with some added secrets revealed. If the ice is dusted with snow, tracks describe the comings and goings of creatures who slip by unnoticed in summer. If the ice freezes quickly, without opaque air bubbles, it makes a clear window to the plants, fishes, and insects below. If it does contain some air bubbles, the thickness of the ice can be judged pretty well at a glance. I stay off ice under two inches thick. I prefer five, when I can get it, since there's no telling how uniform the ice thickness might be with relatively warm springs possible below, currents moving the 33+ degree water about, beavers and their kin chewing holes, and other factors conspiring against rink quality ice.

We also like to combine skating trips with a bit of reconnaissance. If there's a pond or lake we want to explore, a place where the far shore was remote and protected from land access by brush when we forgot the canoe or found it while hiking, ice skating means a good chance to check it out. We tend to choose places with predictably low concentrations of humans, so any trouble we run into, we're on our own. Prior experience in the ways of ice notwithstanding, we packed up spare clothes, a long rope, and the ice axe. No sense regretting them later.

We decided on Hills Pond, an hour or so into the woods between Bald and Tumbledown Mountains. The road should be clear enough for the car, and the studded snow tires would be handy if it was icy. We loaded the skates and other gear, and Kodiak bounded into the back seat. He knows about ice skating.

There was no one at Hills Pond, no tracks down the bank from the road. A snowplow was turning around nearby when we arrived, leaving a good place to park. We were a little disappointed to see snow covering the ice. Wild skating is like fishing; it still requires a bit of luck. But on closer inspection, the snow was only an inch deep. The skates would slide through it, although the snow would cover the flaws like skate-blade eating pressure cracks, and we couldn't just look through it to judge the ice's thickness.

We kept Kodiak leashed and ventured out, tentatively, keeping well apart. So far, so good. David started chipping test holes with the ice axe while I stood ready with the rest of the gear. An ice axe isn't really the best choice for this kind of mining, but we each had one left from earlier forays into ice climbing and glacier travel, and it travels well on a day pack. It also might grip nicely for climbing back on to the ice from below. After a few tries, he abandoned the test holes at four inches each without hitting water. We pronounced the ice not necessarily safe but good enough.

I unleashed Kodiak while David sat on a granite boulder protruding through the ice and pulled on his skates. A fallen log extending diagonally from on the bank to under the ice made a good bench for me. We both wear hockey skates with high tech quick release buckles: no toe teeth to catch on rough surfaces, no fussing with cold hands to get them on or off. Kodiak bounded down the shoreline a few yards and then on to the bank. He'd explore for hours, keeping within our sight while checking out the underbrush, always unsuccessfully.

Hills Pond is a round gem in the mountains ringed with purple flowering rhodora in the summer, and, now, with white shoreline encircled by leatherleaf, balsam fir, handsome black spruce, and towering pines. Although a tall white pine at the far end is said to conceal the high broad nest of a raven, and we'd like to find it, my favorite trees in this place are the black spruce. I admire their northern spirit. Skating with them alone would be worth the trip.

Look where it's colder and wetter, and where there's more wind, and you'll find black spruce. The more wild and rugged, the more shallow the soil, it'll be there. It's in the bogs and swamps, it pioneers boulder fields and survives as a mat on granite mountaintops or on the barrens of the far north. The scraggly, unwavering symbol of the boreal forest.

We rose to our feet and tested the surface of the ice. Smooth enough. No great, long glides, but smooth enough. We skated over to check on Kodiak. He looked like a happy puppy in love with life. He greeted us both and bounded off. We picked just a few of the short spruce needles overhanging the ice and crushed them. They smelled like medicine; black spruce, to be sure. These needles are rarely shed, just a few at a time, an adaptation to harsh living conditions. The little cones do produce seeds, but they're dropped very sparingly unless there's a fire. Since black spruce grow in very marginal places, often standing over seed-smothering mosses, they've also adapted to retaining most of the seeds in their cones until a good, nutrient and sunlight releasing fire comes along. Or, black spruce don't use their seeds at all; seeds are a tough bet for survival in the north. As a more sure method of continued existence, its lower branches can take root when they are covered in moss and ground debris, and a clone grows. That's why a taller spruce will sometimes be surrounded by smaller ones.

We skated cautiously around toward the farthest side of the pond, paralleling the shore. Hidden cracks from the ice expanding or contracting are nothing to take lightly. They run across long expanses and are often just wide enough to catch a skate blade. It seemed unlikely that there would be any so early in the season, but, with the coating of snow, there was no way to tell without a precautionary skate all the way around the pond. Our tracks would at least keep a visual record of where we'd been.

Usually, on the first of January, it is cold. Extremely cold. The ice on our pond has already frozen and expanded by then, reaching its lowest density and maximum buoyancy, and it contracts in the cold, widening and extending any cracks. It talks all night, a long, low "thong", a sound I anticipate every winter like loon calls in summer. Sounds of the North.

David's sister had been skating with us one year, and the bare ice was crisscrossed with spidery lines. The wind was blowing fiercely, and we were bundled up taking advantage of it by skating to one end of the pond and then holding our coats out wide to act as sails. We'd fly all the way back. Unfortunately, each return skate was parallel to most of the cracks in the ice, and, as we grew tired and rubber-kneed, Barb's skateblade dropped into one. I guess she must have involuntarily jerked to free it because both of her feet went forward and high up into the air. In the resulting fall on to the hard ice, the back of her head was the first to hit. One of the only two good things about the whole event was that I was right behind her to see it. It was a truly amazing sight not to be missed. And, with the wind roaring so loudly, she wouldn't have been missed until we turned around on the far side.

I slid on my knees to look at her face. Her eyes were doing odd bouncy motions, like a cartoon character. That didn't seem good. I yelled for David, but the wind blew my words back. I yelled again, as loudly as I could. David glanced back, and Barb woke up, the second good thing. She yelled, too. I couldn't really blame her. We made sure she was okay to be mobile before skating her across the ice, switching to boots, and walking to the house for hot cocoa and a warm fire. After a while, sitting in a safe rocking chair, Barb asked us how she got there. She never did go to the hospital.

We circumnavigated Hills Pond, finding smooth spots on the windless sides and a wonderful absence of cracks, thin ice, and other obstacles. Kodiak seemed preoccupied harmlessly on the shore, not digging, not falling in secret holes. We were ready to stretch out and skate.

There's something very ravenlike about gliding across a boreal pond nestled in the mountains in winter. We may not be quite as graceful as those majestic birds, but the joy of smooth, effortless speed must hint at what they feel, and certainly builds in us the same celebration and play we've seen in them. David tagged me and I raced after him. Every time I skated close, he'd make a sharp, harrier turn, and I'd shoot on by until I made a feint right and skated left, right into his escape path. My turn. He prefers to skate right on my tail, inches back, and we both laugh at how nervous it makes me. On our home ice, I can use his closeness to my advantage and shed him off with a last minute maneuver around a standing tree in the Valley of the Dead. At Hills Pond, I eventually just give.

Kodiak appeared to be behaving just a little too well, still poking along the ice at the shore. We decided to glide over and see what was up. He was glad to show us; he'd had no luck on his own. All along the far shore of the pond, just under the leatherleaf and rhodora, and poking into ever nook and cranny, every boulder crack, every fallen log, ran the tracks of an otter. It had inspected anything and everything interesting, then moved on a bit. In the snow, we could see the marks where it had bounded three or four times, then slid ten or twelve feet on its belly, front legs tucked out of the way but kick marks from its rear feet occassionally showing on either side of the long tail imprinted in the trough-like slide. There seemed to have been only one, and it investigated everything.

We skated along beside Kodiak following the tracks of the curious creature until we found either a hole Kodiak had excavated in the ice for a drink or the otter's passageway to the sub-ice world. Besides mice and other food sources on land, otters eat what they can find underwater, including small fish. They aren't likely to eat trout if they can take dace or perch, slower fish, which they catch by herding several into the shallows under the ice and snatching them there. We inspected the hole but were undecided. We finally found tracks heading into the black spruce and knew the otter was gone. Otters like to den in banks with underwater entrances, but we've heard that they'll also choose a log shelter or another land option. Once, in South Florida, we chanced upon four playing like puppies on an early morning boardwalk.

We resumed skating to warm up. Hills Pond isn't much of a fishing pond, and that isn't why we go there. We usually go for the ravens. A snowshoer in these mountains is often chorused with a "rok" from overhead. In fact, Bernd Heinrich, who studies ravens, has a cabin nearby. We had visited his aviary a couple of years ago. Heinrich's studies have shown ravens are as clever and as mischievous as their reputations report.

While Hills Pond may not be an angler's lake, ravens have taken advantage of ice fishermen in other places. There's a recent Scandinavian story about a winter angler who left his bait suspended from a cord attached to a stick spanning his fishing hole. Every day, he'd return to the ice to find his fish stolen, until he finally saw the culprit. A raven pulled the stick from across the hole and laid it to one side. Then the raven pulled more of the cord up with its beak, secured the cord with its foot, and repeated the steps until it had the fish.

Heinrich tested ravens in his aviary on a similar principle. From a clothesline, he hung two cords, one supporting a rock and one a piece of meat. Each raven would peer down at the problem from its perch on the clothesline. Then with beak and foot would pull up the correct cord every time. Taking the experiment one step farther, he crossed the cords suspending the rock and the meat, anchoring them apart with an invisible line. A raven perched over the cord attached to the meat would look down to see the stone below. The ravens got it right.

Based on tests including brain cavity capacity, Heinrich estimated that a raven's brain volume is about twice that of a crow and over five times that of a chicken (never assumed to be intellectual giants on our farm). Crows, incidentally, never did solve even the first clothesline puzzle. We've since heard that ravens have roughly the equivalent intelligence to their long-time partners, wolves and coyotes. And dogs. I looked across the pond at Kodiak, who looks a bit like a coyote with floppy ears. He was still searching for the otter. Sometimes I wonder.

Somewhere, up over Kodiak, high in one of the towering white pines, Heinrich had written of a raven's nest. We've looked for it from shore and from the ice, and we've never found it. Maybe it's gone, or maybe he was protecting its location, like a good angler protects a favorite pool on a productive stream. In a way, we're just as happy we couldn't find it. Ravens mate for life, just like beavers do, and are thought to live about forty years. If we can't find the nest, then there's hope that no one else will find it, and the pair can enjoy many more years of relative security. With that as a parting thought, we leashed our tired canine friend and skated toward the car. By the time we had our skates off and our gear stowed, he was asleep on the back seat.

Det-thlok

"Finally, snow so deep that snowshoes are necessary....."

Ⅰ'd been buried in field guides all morning, but, by eleven, the snow was too much for Kodiak and me to resist. I decided we'd head out. Yesterday's storm had come in the night and hurried on by morning. Some wind had followed during the day, so today was technically the second day after the storm and looked like it. The sky was an endless blue, and the brilliant sun, at such a low angle, made long contrasting shadows on the white snow.

Det-thlok, finally. Snow so deep that snowshoes are necessary to move through it, a word attributed to the Inuit. Whether or not the word is actually used in the far north, I couldn't say, but I liked it the second I heard it. It was perfect. I needed a word like that.

I checked the thermometer. It had risen from the pre-dawn 10 degrees to just above 30 degrees. If I kept to the shade, it might be cold enough to keep the snow from balling up in the cleats under the pivoting binding of my featherweight snowshoes. The shorter, lighter snowshoes would be fine with only nine inches of relatively buoyant powder overlying the twelve that had settled for two weeks. I wanted shoes that could make just a bit of difference in case I traveled over snow supported by small firs or brush, but not so heavy they'd slow me down or wear me out breaking trail. These were eight inches wide, thirty inches long. We were headed for the woods and didn't need any extra length to get tangled in the trees. This type, narrow with a slight tail, is called both the Maine and the Michigan style, a coincidence that makes me smile. We use them in both states.

At thirty degrees, the sun would feel hot with the hard work of breaking trail but the shady woods would be cool. I still couldn't completely trust the ice, now snow-covered and both insulated and hidden from inspecting eyes. The beavers would be chewing it from below, exhaling carbon dioxide and releasing oxygen bubbles from their coats all along their channels. The warmer water underneath the ice and the out gases of plant decomposition make me distrust our congested pools. Better to stay off the center ice and stick to the shade for the most part. I could test the ice depths near shore.

Choosing what to wear depends on a combination of the activity about to be undertaken and the weather but also requires a brief nod to what could happen. Dave Norling, a bamboo rodmaker from Minnesota, wrote that there is no bad weather, just bad clothes. It pays to consider what to wear. If Kodiak fell through the ice, I could end up wetter than deep snow or good, hard effort might predict. The trick is to stay warm but ventilated, wear layers for on-the-trail adjustments, and be ready for an unlikely but still potential soaking. Synthetic fleece and wool are both warm when wet.

I decided to pull on light pile pants and a polypropylene turtleneck with a neck zipper vent. I chose waterproof wind pants instead of gaiters so I could sit down anywhere and rest and so I could shed snow dumped by low hanging branches along my bushwhacking route. Thirty degrees and breaking trail meant that just a wool sweater and a hooded wind breaker would be enough of an outer layer to keep me comfortable, ventilated, and warm if wet.

I found a thick pair of mittens, wool socks, and a pile hat to wear and put a second set in my daypack, along with a compass, water bottle, the 100-foot rescue rope, and sunscreen for my lips and nose. My sunglasses were a given; I wear them whenever I'm out in the winter sun. I pulled the handle of my ice axe up through the haul loop on the top of the pack and flipped it back over to hang down behind me, secured at the head by the inverted loop. Kodiak's leash was hanging on the doorknob. I tucked it into my pack, too, but then had to deal with a mildly exploding dog while I laced up my hiking boots.

I opened the door, and he rocketed past the startled chickadees on the feeders. I made a mental note that their sunflower seeds were almost gone, and the timing would be right for chickadee games when we returned.

My snowshoes were already outside, cold. I lifted my right foot into the securing straps first and pulled the cord which tightens the binding over the arch of that foot. Then I brought the back strap up over my heel and pulled it tight. I tied the ends of the two straps loosely together so they wouldn't dangle under my snowshoes, tripping me or wearing under the cleats. One quick yank and they could be untied. Two more yanks and the snowshoes could be jettisoned in brushpile tangles or deep water.

With my right snowshoe on, I transferred my weight to that dominant foot and repeated the process with my left. This technique isn't as necessary with snowshoes as it is with ice skates, but it helps with balance and allows me to shoe up quickly.

Kodiak came back to watch me strap on my snowshoes and see which way we were headed. I smiled at him, eye to eye, and signaled north with my mitten. He ran into the canoe shed, out through the other side, and off toward the north house. I met him waiting on the steps, ears cocked and wondering if we were going in or onward.

"This way," I said, pointing north. He led the way through the gap in the stone wall; I followed, breaking a new trail. We dropped into the North Marsh together. I was getting warmed up. The marsh grasses had held up under the snow, making a series of faux hummocks, mounds which looked solid but certainly weren't. Every step had to be raised to their height. Then my weight would crush the snow-covered grass back down. It wasn't hard going, but it was work. I was getting hot.

We emerged from the woods for a moment at the north end of the chain of ponds. I rested where I could see them stretching south, a sparkling snow covered expanse broken occasionally by the line of a beaver dam and outlined by dark balsam fir that rose up the ridges of Hampshire Hill toward the flawless sky. The sun may have been in its low winter arc, but that didn't keep it from turning the new snow into diamonds or from feeling warm on my cheeks.

At the stream, I was pleased to see that enough snow had fallen to make little banks that nearly touched from one side of the stream to the other. The stream was low yet from summer, the water so shallow that the penalty for a missed jump was worth the risk compared to the hassle of removing my snowshoes to wade across. I tested the grip of my cleats, then pushed off with my right foot and landed successfully on my left.

Kodiak crossed on the dam and came to meet me as I entered the woods. It was time to see if I could remember the landmarks leading to the old foundations without using the compass in my daypack. I had the sun to my left, the distant noise of skidders to my right, and the inspiration of an incredible day to carry me on. I took off my hat and mittens, put them in the daypack, and then pointed west into the woods. "This way," I told him.

Elevated a foot by snow that had fallen since our last trek through this area, I had more trouble with overhanging branches than with landmarks. The height of the snowpack in February would be a good time for trimming trails; the offenders would be within reach. I made note of which ones would have to go as I ducked under hemlocks toward the isolated cherry, right on course. From there, we dropped to a narrow alder swamp, catkins still clinging and unbroken on the twigs. I heard harmless little snaps under the snow, ice breaking under my feet. My snowshoes would span any water there, but the snaps were still interesting to hear. Probably the water level had been higher when the ice formed, and there were air pockets under it now that the water level was lower, denying the ice any real support.

We emerged at the back of the granite foundations, listened for the friendly ghosts of cattle and horses from a century or two before, and then turned north on to the snowmobile trail. My snowshoes clattered on its hard surface. Around the corner, we stepped into the deeper snow of the woods and trudged westward to the snow-covered springholes at the base of the West Ridge. Then we started up. By packing long switchbacks, I traveled twice as far but was half as tired as Kodiak, who bounded straight up and then waited for me, panting. We explored the top of the ridge for deer and partridge tracks, none present since the new snow, then followed the ridgetop south before dropping down and re-accessing the snowmobile trail.

Continuing on the reverse loop from the evening Kodiak had disappeared digging, we only had to cross the trail and we would be back on the linking trail to our pond. Instead, I pretended to be very interested in an old standing tree trunk, pecked full of round downy woodpecker holes as deep as a forefinger could measure. Kodiak came over to investigate, as hoped, and I leashed him up. If we were going to walk back on the edge of the pond, I wanted to assure he wouldn't be running out to the beaver lodges and falling in an air hole. He was tired and just as glad to pass dominance to me for a leisurely walk down the linking trail.

When we stepped out of the sheltering trees on to the Big Pond, the contrast hit us, sparkling white, flat and open, a Florida beachwalk. The low sun was still beating down with amazing strength, and the snow reflected sunlight upward. I stopped to put sunscreen on my nose, then traded venting my sweater and turtle-neck in the warmth for pulling my mittens back on. I was 99% sure we wouldn't fall through the ice, but that was no reason to be careless or lazy. It only took a minute to dig the mittens out of the daypack and insure that my hands would be warm in ice water. I left my hat packed away. If the ice cracked, I wanted to hear it.

We dawdled the length of the pond as we traveled south from Bull Moose Cove. There was leatherleaf protruding through the snow on the stumps still rising above the ice. Mink tracks bounded from the shore to the beaver lodge, but leashbound Kodiak couldn't follow them. Deer tracks paralleled ours, and chickadees sang in the firs just feet away on the shore. I glanced across the pond to our house perched above. Feeder birds often commute great distances so they can retain rights to their breeding ranges. I wondered if I'd be seeing these westside chickadees when I was on the east side, at the feeders by our back door.

I decided to leave the ice at Duck Cove and avoid crossing the long beaver channel I knew was hidden in the Valley of the Dead.

David and I had once found a very large hole in the channel ice and the snowy tracks leading from it where a moose had shaken off after its inadvertent bath. The detour would add a quarter mile to the snowshoeing, but we were in no hurry, and it would be nice to get the entire float packed. Snowshoe trails may be packed depressions, but one misstep into the deeper snow on either side makes them seem like floats, floating rafts above the water. Or, in deep winter, above bottomless snow. Kodiak led the way to the Grass Dam, still leashed, but he was too tired to mine for the ever-elusive mink when we crossed it. He was an appropriately pooped pooch when we arrived home.

This was the chance I had been waiting for. Two hours had been enough for the chickadees to empty both feeders. I packed the deep snow under the feeders, shook off my snowshoes, and let Kodiak inside, where he headed straight up to our bed. I dropped the daypack and scooped up a container of black oil sunflower seeds, manna from chickadee heaven. I was hot from snowshoeing, and a little chickadee training would be just right for the cool down.

Black-capped chickadees overwinter with both good humor and clever adaptations to the season, traits I admire. They are friendly, curious, and amused by things like bugs burrowing under bark and humans with snowshoes or a handful of seeds. I've always felt that if you can't enjoy winter, you should migrate south.

There are tricks to enjoying winter, and half of them involve being comfortable, knowing how to dress to stay warm and dry. Chickadees manage to do it despite their small size. Larger birds, like ravens and great horned owls, have greater mass compared to the surface area of their bodies so they lose less heat than the diminutive chickadee. The little birds may cool off much faster than the larger birds, but they've developed counter measures. Chickadees are able to find hidden bug larvae and to locate tiny seeds and nuts in secret places. To work this hard, they have a high metabolic rate that warms them as long as this high-test fuel lasts. I used to worry about chickadees growing dependent on our bird feeders, especially when filled with such a high-energy food as black oil sunflowers. While it seems a humane way of helping them through the winter, was there an inherent harm?

I had talked to Herb Wilson, a local biology professor, about chickadees and feeder dependence. He went far into the North Woods of Maine, where det-thlok comes early, and established a series of chickadee feeding stations. As I understand it, the first two and the last one he stocked immediately with seeds, but he held off on the third. As time went by, he stopped supplying the first, and started at the third. The second he stopped stocking later when he resumed the seed supply at the first. The second was resumed when he stopped the third. The fourth he kept stocked all season. He banded birds at all of the stations and maybe even at a fifth station where no seeds were ever stocked.

What he found is that chickadees will come to feeders when that food source is available, but there don't appear to be any appreciable dependency or depredation effects on the birds. As I remember, he also found that there are eight to ten times as many chickadees coming to a feeder as there appears to be at any one time. Count the chickadees you see, multiply by ten.

Our feeders are long tubes that hang from a two-crooked shepherd's staff made of wrought iron. Just beyond the feeders are two wild hazelnuts, shrubs that provide some cover and many twigs serving as chickadee launch sites. The hazelnuts are sheltered from above by a white birch, natural habitat for many birds, and on the west by balsam fir. Chickadees zoom into the secret places of the dense firs from all directions, narrowly missing our heads when we wander into their flight paths. They fly into the birch to survey the situation, then drop into the hazelnuts for the final approach.

With my sunglasses masking my eyes, I stood near the shepherd's crook, extending a hand heaped with seeds. I braced my forearm against the iron so I could hold my offering adjacent to an empty feeder tube, motionless, for as long as it took. The sunglasses hide my eyes; our chickadees seem shyer if stared at. A shaky hand doesn't help, either. Still warm, well-braced, eyes shielded, I was ready for the long haul. I waited with my offering.

The first person I had ever seen feed chickadees by hand was Vera Neuman, a retired teacher and naturalist who lived near our Michigan farm. Her glassed-in front porch was cluttered with all sorts of good stuff when I was too little to reach most of it: a salamander in a well-developed terrarium, preserved snakes coiled in jars, a large paperwasp's nest, turtle eggs. My older brother and I loved to visit her. She taught us to make maple syrup candy and to observe the world under our noses. Her chickadees loved her.

The flutter of curious chickadees is like magic. Out of the corner of my averted eyes I could see two, then eight, looking me over, cocking their little heads. I tried not to smile. The timid flew off, the bold flew closer. A couple talked to me. "Dee-dee-dee?" they asked, politely. I waited. The first one flew to the feeder, tagged up, and flew back to the hazelnut. So far, so good. The second sounded like it did the same; it was beyond my view. I resisted my curiosity and waited, conscious of a dozen little souls testing me.

We were in the shadows, and they looked chubby. Like most birds, a chickadee can fluff its feathers and make a little down jacket of trapped air for insulation. When it gets colder, the blood vessels on the surface of its feet and legs shrink, cutting down on blood flow and therefore on heat loss. We put up a roost for them, an insulated box full of small perches with a chickadee sized hole near the bottom. We'd hoped to help them through cold nights and storms, but a red squirrel adopted the roost box for its own, and the chickadees seem to do fine huddling in the spruce and fir, so we let the squirrel retain possession. I've heard that chickadees are capable of constantly shivering and that it multiples their metabolic rate five times. As long as the food/fuel holds out, they're warm.

No wonder these were getting bolder. The third daring chickadee landed on my little finger's tip, nabbed a seed, and fluttered off, and a forth took heart and copied him. They have a surprisingly gentle grip and weigh almost nothing. I'd been lost in chickadees, but slowly became aware of Kodiak in the background, a muffled demand for liberation. The UPS truck was driving in, probably with a ferrule order. I tipped the seeds from my hand into the top of the nearest tube, filled both from the container at my feet, and went to check.

The Wood-burning Cookstove

"The patents cast into the left end, near the dampers, speak of Boston and 1898."

The house is still standing and the food tasted great, so I guess my first attempt with a turn of the century (the last one) wood burning cookstove was successful. Every romantic vision of returning from the outdoors to hot coffee, potatoes fried to just about golden brown, and fresh bread from the oven, all heated skillfully by a nostalgic combination of cast iron cookery and wood from the stack near the door starts, I suspect, with the same step. How do I work this thing?

The kitchen in the north house was designed with a country feel. There are wooden beams once adorned with antiques and hanging herbs, tongue and groove pine cupboards, and an offset, open dining area with large sliding glass doors overlooking the Big Dam and the North Pond and across to Bull Moose Cove. Deer pick their way across the dam on early spring mornings, and moose wade in the cove on summer evenings. Now, with the world frozen and beautiful, I can stand in the dining room and just make out coyote tracks traveling down the length of the northern pond, over the dam and beyond. Comfortably commanding the west wall, opposite the cupboards and adjacent to the dining area, a stately black cast iron cookstove is the centerpiece of the kitchen.

I was lucky to be in good company. David's mom, Dorothy, was still in Maine and game to try. At least she had used one before, albeit seventy years or so ago. We laughed about having trouble remembering details from yesterday, let alone seven decades ago, but I was thinking that wood cookstoves might be a little like bicycles. Once we started, I hoped it would all come back.

The stove is a Crawford Century, and the patents cast into the left end, near the dampers, speak of Boston and 1898. David had printed a drawing of this very stove from the internet, anatomically labeled, and we used the sketch to systematically inspect our subject. If there were going to be problems, we resolved to discover them before we lit a match. And before we'd had a chance to remodel the place and move in.

Standing in front of the stove, we found the door to the firebox. We had heard that the stove had last been used as emergency heat during the Ice Storm, the weather event with capital letters six Januarys before but still a vivid memory. It must have worked then, we decided. At least to some extent. To the right of the firebox was the large oven door, complete with white, circular, inset thermometer. That door also opened freely, with the characteristic cast iron creak of a woodstove door. There was an intact rack inside. The water tank was next, left to right, but since it opened on top of the stove, we left the tank for later and moved up to surface of the stove, again beginning on the left.

Two burners were directly over the firebox, and their plates could be lifted out to reveal the eventual flames below. Four more circular burner plates were over the oven. To the far right on the surface of the stove, the top of the water tank was intact and opened with no problem. The deep, dark tank was empty and didn't appear rusted, but light shown in at the bottom. There was a drain hole, unplugged. We paused to consider that.

"Do you think we can run the stove without water in here?" I asked Dorothy, peering inside. I wasn't eager to deal with the missing plug, the potential for rust, or a lot of leftover hot water we really didn't need.

"Oh, sure," she said, riding her bicycle.

Still on the stove's surface but at the very back of the stove, above the back end of the firebox, was a slider made of cast iron. The left end of the slide was labeled "bake", the middle was labeled "check", and the right end was labeled "kindle". Dorothy tried it, sliding the knob to "kindle". No problem. Sliders on the left end of the stove, on the side, also worked. The lower one was the damper, which we opened, and the upper one was for using coal. We left that one closed.

The cast iron support for the chimney extended from the back of the stove, in the center. There was a small, ornate warming shelf on either side. Each could be rotated over the burners and oven for more heat or rotated all of the way around to the back of the stove for less heat. Another solid shelf was above them where the chimney exited the cast iron, turned with a 90 degree elbow, and disappeared into a square of bricks trimmed with pine.

So far, so good.

Dorothy volunteered to dig out the ashes from the firebox. After I found her the small shovel and ash bucket, I moved through the entrance foyer into the open living room and turned down the thermostat to shut down the furnace and free the kitchen chimney. Then I started a good fire in the Jotul on the new brick hearth in the still mostly empty living room. We'd need some heat if our little project didn't work out. By then, Dorothy was ready for the Shop Vac, and I dragged it over.

The last thing I expected when vacuuming the remnant ashes out of an 1898 wood fired cookstove was the stinging snap of an electric shock, so much so that I immediately tried it again. The second shock proved to us that the first wasn't a fluke. After the third, I called David. Besides being a bamboo rodmaker, he has a background in both mechanical engineering and physics. Maybe even a little metallurgy. He can be useful.

After a brief discussion of dust particles, static electricity, exploding grain elevators, and our relative safety, Dorothy and I were back at it. The stove looked beautiful, black, shiny, and ready. I brought up a load of kindling, and we seemed to be ready, too. We both giggled a little. I decided to read the instructions on the fire extinguisher. Dorothy wiped the stovetop with a paper towel while I studied. The bank had given us the fire extinguisher as a gift when we bought this house, although I was pretty sure there was no hidden meaning implied. Dorothy held her paper towel for me to see; it was a greasy, solid black. Stove blacking? Grease? We looked around for the plant mister. We had one somewhere; we'd plan to use to spray the downstairs wallpaper to loosen it. Spraying a mist of water into a stove works well, we'd heard, for chimney fires.

Then, we couldn't think of anything else to do, so we crumpled some newspaper in the firebox, piled on kindling, and lit our match.

The newspaper accepted the tiny flame and nurtured it into enough of a fire to light the kindling. Smoke began to pour out through the burners. We looked at each other.

"That's not supposed to happen," Dorothy said, cracking a window.

We checked the draft on the stove – open. There was no draft on the chimney, so we didn't see how it could be closed. The flames of the newspaper licked higher, then died back as the wood took over. Less smoke was coming into the room.

"Maybe it's not hot enough to draw well," I offered.

It seemed plausible to both of us. I blew on the wood, and then we decided to add more. We were in this now, come what may.

As the wood turned to bright coals, and we kept adding more, the smoke diminished. We opened another window and turned on a fan, proud of ourselves. Evidently, we had this stove under control. For thirty minutes or more, we chatted about woodstoves and cooking and fed wood to the Jotul in the living room and back to the kitchen to feed the Crawford. And back to the Jotul, which was getting toasty; the thermometer said 400 degrees, just right. And back to the Crawford. The oven thermometer hadn't moved.

"Maybe it's broken," I said.

Dorothy opened the oven door and felt inside. Pretty cool. Then she remembered the slider at the back of the firebox and switched it over to "bake". We giggled more over forgetting it already; good thing no one but Kodiak was there to see us.

Within a few minutes, two things happened. The oven temperature gauge stated climbing, and the house began filling with smoke again. It seemed like smoke was pouring from all four burners above the oven.

"Well", Dorothy laughed through the haze, "at least the oven is getting hot."

We were both a little nervous but even more curious. We looked at the surface of the stove carefully, examining the pattern of the smoke. It had stopped rising on the left, nearest the firebox, and those burner plates were more gray than black. That gray seemed to be following the diminishing smoke across the surface of the stove. Was the culprit stove blacking?

Within an hour, the stove was less pretty but behaving well, and we decided to move on to the next step: cooking. I crossed to the counter and surveyed the room, then went into the dining room to look back.

"Is there much smoke?" Dorothy asked, watching me. We were both pretty used to it, like in an old log cabin camping on a winter night.

I couldn't believe the haze.

We opened windows the length of the house, turned on the fan, stoked both fires, and set to preparing the food. Dorothy had thawed the venison she'd carried from Michigan on the warming shelf of the Crawford, and it was ready to go. She sliced potatoes to fry while I mixed a batch of corn bread. We put two cast iron fry pans, one large and one small, and a cast iron muffin pan on the stovetop to warm.

Watching the clock, Dorothy started the potatoes first, our most expendable experiment. She used a spatula to drop margarine in the small pan. It sizzled nicely. Then the sliced potatoes. We watched them together for a minute. Not too hot but hot enough. She prepared the second fry pan for the venison hamburgers. When that margarine sizzled, she slid the potatoes back to the rear burner plate over the firebox and used the front one. The venison roused Kodiak from a sound sleep, and he re-positioned himself in the kitchen.

Meanwhile, the temperature gauge on the oven slowly rose. I added wood and watched it. Cornbread muffins are usually baked at 400 degrees, but at 300 degrees we pronounced the oven ready enough for us and slid in the filled muffin pan.

I went outside to get bigger firewood for the Jotul while Dorothy watched our supper. It'd be nice to put a long-lasting log or two on the fire and settle back in front of it for supper with David. Beginning Monday, I'd lose the freedom of my brief sabbatical, and woodstoves would become an evening or weekend pleasure again. While I was outside, Dorothy inspected the house. The contrast between the fresh air I had let in and our smoky ambience was still a bit dramatic, so she opened more windows.

We were both giggling a little when I added more logs to the Jotul and almost missed checking the muffins. Dorothy snatched them out, golden brown. Neither one of us was waiting for David with these. Dorothy lifted one gingerly out of the pan and pulled it in half. It melted in our mouths like the best food we'd ever eaten.

Four were gone by the time David arrived. We had mastered jockeying the pans around the stovetop to keep the food warmed just so and were letting the firebox coals die out. We had closed some of the windows and turned on the light over the front door to welcome him.

The three of us settled in front of the Jotul's sweet, simmering logs to eat, Dorothy on the only chair, David on a milk crate, me sitting next to Kodiak on his dog bed. It was just over eighty degrees in the house.

"So, everything went okay?" David asked. I felt a little guilty that he had been left out.

"It went okay," his mom said, with a quick wink my way.

"Do we smell smoky?" I asked.

"Should you?" he asked.

The Ice Storm

"Electric lines were down, road crews were losing ground and there was more yet to come!"

On the first of February, at midnight and again at 3 a.m., Kodiak had to go out. We used the occasions to check the storm's progress. It wasn't living up to the dire predictions, and hadn't still at 5:30. We flicked on the television and heard the "Storm Center" theme music, so I propped myself up on an elbow to check the scrolling names at the bottom of the screen. My school was in the long list, but David's district hadn't thrown in the towel yet. They had a faculty workshop scheduled so no students would be at risk at the roadsides. He dressed and went out to investigate, and I shifted my attention from the sounds of the tv banter to the muffled pinging resonating down the stovepipe. Windows, too.

"Sleet?" I asked as he came in, stamping off a little snow at the door.

"Needles," he said, "but not bad. They plowed the road, but not down to the surface."

They, in this case, are neighbors who have the road contract locally. Each March at the town meeting, we all gather at the school after a community supper to decide the budget and put in our two cents' worth on local issues, as well as renew old acquaintances and get all the news. The New England town meeting is a great old system that keeps faces on government officials and makes us all responsible for our collective decisions. It works well for the roads; the guy behind the wheel of the plow or sand truck is sitting right there, fair game. It's his choice whether he hears praise or criticism, determined on days like today. With predictions turning now to sleet (rain freezing as it falls) or freezing rain (rain freezing on contact with cold objects, roads, power lines), leaving some accumualtion on the road would mitigate the slipperiness and makes the roads easier to plow since the crust can be scraped off with the snow. Otherwise, the cleared road surface could coat with ice and stay that way until sand, salt, and sun could melt it. He's a smart guy, and I'll tell him so next month. I'll leave the snow on the decks and walkways until the weather clears, too.

David decided to take the truck as long as snow was more of a consideration than ice, four wheel drive preferable to the greater control on ice offered by the car's studded tires. With any luck, the road would be cleared and sanded by night. I'd call him in an hour, just to double check that he made it okay and to get the detailed scouting report.

The night before we had filled the bird feeders with black oil sunflower seeds and refilled our cache of water, then relaxed. I'm afraid that for a lot of people in Maine it was an anxious night, and I can't blame them. The weatherman had said ice was coming, and it seemed like everyone had heard him. While I hoped the approaching storm would be kinder than predicted, the word was bleak. It was coming from Oklahoma, usually perceived as light years away from Maine, but the news said that they'd been coated with ice for three days and power was out in a dozen counties now declared national disaster areas. It struck a discordant note. A few years ago, it had been Maine's turn.

In 1998, we returned from the holidays in Michigan to fifty-degree temperatures on Saturday, January 3rd. It was wonderfully warm and sunny the next day, so we worked on the roof of the canoe shed in shirtsleeves, clearing it of the eight inches of snow which had fallen while we were gone. We dried our Christmas laundry on the clothesline outside. I sat for a while on the deck, hoping the sun would freshen my stuffy head like it freshened the clothes on the line. We had driven over 2,000 miles in seven days and packed those days full of whirlwind visits to friends and family. Someone must have had a cold.

Monday turned cloudy and damp. I reentered the world of kids and school feeling like I was submerged in a great incubator of cold germs and was basically doomed. I went to bed early that night, marveling to the drumming of rain on the roof. It was cold, 27 degrees at ground level. High above, it was much warmer. The rain fell all night and continued as a mist in the morning. Every surface it touched was colder, still 27 degrees. We were coated with a thin layer of ice.

We made our way to school in the Kennebec River Valley where the ice coating hadn't progressed quite as far, but it was misty all day, and the trip home was slick. Every twig, every power line, glistened. It was beautiful. I gave up on Wednesday and tried to call in sick to spare my students and colleagues from my cold germs only to find that school had been canceled. It was still 27 degrees, but pellets of ice were falling. David had to go in, but I had full license to hibernate, and Kodiak kept me company. He insisted on rousting me to let him out in the early afternoon but changed his mind at the door. I wore my rain gear to replenish the bird feeders and put out suet. David made it home before dark. It was 24 degrees when we went to bed, and the forecast was for freezing rain and ice.

By Thursday, January 8th, all of the schools were canceled. The forecast was accurate. We watched out the windows as the twigs grew thicker and imagined the weight on the power lines. None were visible from our snug vantage point, but the scenes on television were growing more dramatic. Electric lines were snapping, road crews were losing ground, and there was more yet to come. We had our camping gear, food, water, a multitude of light sources (headlamps, kerosene lamp, flashlights, candles), and a good stash of firewood. I had a perfect reason to stay in bed all day and sleep off my cold. We watched in awe and waited.

The power went out at noon. We switched to the Walkman portable radio and phoned Barb to make sure she was okay. When a state of emergency was declared at 2 pm, we decided to call home. We were fine and thought we'd better let our parents know it before they heard on the six o'clock news that Maine was in trouble. Luck was with us. We made contact with Mom and Archie in Florida and Dad, Sue, and Dorothy in Michigan before the phone went dead at 3 p.m. The wood stove created a soft orange glow, and I was personally very happy to go to bed at dark.

On Friday morning, we refueled the coals in the wood stove, reached for the orange juice stashed in the cooler-turned-squirrel-proof-refrigerator just outside the back door, and surveyed the situation. There was three quarters of an inch of ice coating every-thing. Each twig was as thick as a crystal hot dog. The birches lining our drive bent low to the ground, blocking any hope of passage. The deck was coated as thickly, and the ice capping the snow extended all across our clearing. I walked on it trying to convince Kodiak to extend his range a bit farther from the house, but he chose the slope near the back door to squat down, then went into a slow slide and spin while he was taking care of business. He had a sheepish look clawing his way back to the house and remained unconvinced. We decided to stay put, and I spent the day back in bed pampering the last vestiges of my cold, luxury amidst disaster.

On Saturday, there were patches of blue sky at 8 a.m., and it was sunny and 35 degrees by 10:30. The phone was working, and Barb was fine. We went for a walk wearing snowshoes with cleats for traction on the icy crust. We kept to the pond and waterways as much as possible, avoiding the slopes and the jungle of hanging branches and bent saplings. Arched treetops and strained limbs were anchored under the icy snow blocking all of our snowshoe trails, and the alder thickets were impassable. But the sun was wonderful, and the world was intensely bright. We put on our sunglasses and unzipped our parkas. From out on the pond, we listened to the crashes of ice falling in the woods as the sun worked its magic. Where trees had sheltered the crust it was thinner and succumbed to the warmth quicker. Saplings bent double, tips trapped in the crust's grip, would suddenly spring free, and the shock shattered the ice coating every branch. It crashed on to the icy crust below with the incredible sound of breaking glass. The melody was complemented by the percussion snaps of limbs whenever the ice coating melted past the point of providing structural support and became dead, limb breaking weight. Occasionally, there was a rifle shot crack as a tree finally lost to the weight of the ice. We stayed out of the woods.

That night, the moon came out and our clearing was intensely beautiful, nearly as light as day. Still, no power had been restored. What progress had been made was thwarted by falling ice, rebounding branches, and snapping trees. We had the wanigan, our kitchen-in-a-box for camping, out and fully operational. By the light of the Aladdin lamp and the glow of the woodstove, we had the wooden lid flipped open, swinging the single burner stove into place upright. David removed the canister of propane from storage in the box and attached it to the hose leading to the burner. He filled a pan with water from the one on the woodstove where we were keeping a supply of melting snow. No sense breaking into the stored water unless we had to. We readied hot cocoa and coffee to go with cheese sandwiches and considered the problem of listening to basketball.

University of Maine's women's basketball, to be specific.

One of our former students, Cindy Blodgett, had led our high school to an amazing four consecutive class A basketball championships. She was unassuming, hard working, dedicated, and genuine, and the entire state grew to love her. She had decided to go to the University of Maine, much to everyone's delight, choosing home state loyalty over personal opportunity. Maine loved her even more. Even homestate author Stephen King noticed her, and he and Tabitha followed Cindy through high school to college, adding just that much more excitement to the games. Somehow, even without electricity, we knew that the state would be listening to the game, if there was a game.

We had one Walkman, and neither of us wanted to lapse into isolated listening if we could enjoy a cozy evening together. We hit upon the idea of attaching the battery-powered speakers from the computer to the Walkman and came back into contact with the outside world.

Over the next few days, we'd listen to Mainers with power offering their homes, incredibly, over the air to anyone who needed a shower or a safe haven, to recipes for removing candlewax from table linens, and to non-electric games children with cabin fever might enjoy. We heard that Cindy had an injury and that someone was speculating, tongue-in-cheek, that the news had reached the state's most famous author and number one fan just before the Ice Storm hit. That theory was mentioned later in Sports Illustrated, much to everyone's amazement and greater amusement.

Sunday was ice-beautiful, glorious in the sun, and glittering. By noon the temperature was well above freezing and there was another spectacular show of shattering, crashing ice. We surveyed the road, clear and well-sanded, and speculated about getting the vehicles out. The radio said the National Guard preferred to have cars off the road in town and to the south, but the mountains had been spared the ice. We were in the foothills, the dividing line. Maybe tomorrow we'd go see. David ran the snowblower, and I shook the birches to shed their remaining icy weight and then helped them rebound out of the way.

My cold was gone, and we were both fine. We were enjoying soup by firelight and had already put away the wanigan for the night when, at 7:30, the lights came on. They'd been out 79 hours.

We were lucky.

We flicked on the television, found a station which worked, and learned that 270,000 were still without power. The National Guard was trying to clear trees in most of the towns, and power crews from several states away had come to help work on the lines. Amazingly, people were doing pretty well. A lot of Mainers have wood stoves, many have generators, and most are campers at heart. As it turned out, the bulk of the real casualties were psychological.

From the start, we were aware of the restless out there cruising. We'd see them drive by, or they'd drop in to see if we wanted to go to town. People who rarely stay home, who like to see what's going on, who turn on the television and leave it on all day, who check their e-mail constantly, who go out for every meal, or the ones who thrive on crowds, those people suffered more than the elderly and the shut-ins, who had legitimate need for power but kept a stiff upper lip.

People who need a shower every day and who depend on the schools to amuse their children learned a lot about austerity and about family. People who worry, worried. People who can't wait, waited. For them, things were difficult.

For them, the rest of the state came through. It seemed like every home was open, power or not, if someone else needed food, shelter, or the comfort of good company. Generators were unplugged and hefted into pick-up beds, mobile jolts of electricity for thawing freezers or freezing furnaces. Parents traded entertaining groups of each other's children with good old-fashioned games; their own parents were called upon for a refresher in the rules. Teenagers toured neighborhoods to pick up fallen limbs and make friends with the young volunteers of the National Guard, whose jeeps and humvees were parked anywhere help was needed. The soup kitchens weren't the only ones making and delivering meals. Good deeds are good therapy for those who wait.

The waiting did seem to go on and on. We actually thought we might have school that Monday, but it hadn't really sunk in that we were living at the milder northern edge of the storm. Entire trunk lines were gone in Down East Maine, and a senator was exploring bringing in an aircraft carrier for its generators and helping hands. All week we watched the numbers: 140,000 still out, 120,000. The temperatures dipped to 8 degrees, and there were still 62,000 homes without power. By the weekend, there were still 36,000.

Then, on Martin Luther King, Jr., Day, January 19th, we heard that the emergency shelters in the nearby schools were no longer needed and would be disinfected before school the next day. We went back to work, driving in past twenty-five miles of skeletons of pines, maples split in half, and birches snapped in two. Some of the stories were amazing: kids moving downed electric lines off mailboxes to check for mail, families who had lost the food in their refrigerators. Everyone who could make it to school, did, and we were all glad to be back, but the Ice Storm overshadowed every lesson at first. We talked about wrapping cold food in an insulating material, like newspaper, and putting it out in the shadiest snow. We talked about the role of the National Guard.

As nearly as I could tell, the most trying, wearisome, agonizing days of the past weeks were those when the unknown loomed and 'what next?' went unanswered. Will a short cause a fire? Will the roof hold the weight? For the kids, will we have to make up fourteen days of school? Our friends in town felt the loss of those things they always had day to day: movies, shops, places to go, things to do. By contrast, Ruth and Clifford, the elderly couple at the far end of Barb's dead end road, had lived on their farm fifty-five years before there was power. They welcomed the town fathers who had made their way in to the rescue via four wheel drive by offering them a piece of Ruth's freshly baked pie and homemade baked beans. Clifford and Ruth were pleased and surprised to have company but were even more surprised when they learned of the mission's original purpose.

The week at work wore on, and people were worn out. Many still had no power at home, ten days, eleven, twelve, thirteen. They were too worn out by Friday, with 3,500 outages remaining, to hear the new forecast: more freezing rain, the last straw. As I left school on Friday, one of the teachers I admire the most was crying. More freezing rain. Then on Sunday, 70,000 were without power.

We weren't hit so hard the second time, not like the people on the coast, but the one-two punch drove the lessons home. The second storm retaught us that sometimes we have no real control, that being unprepared or letting things slide has consequences, and that we can learn to handle almost anything. When the ice layered snow slid off the roof in the first spring thaw and punched a fist-sized hole in the chimney, we combined learning to repair the roof with a resolve to keep a closer eye on the snow accumulating there. When the snow melted in mid March, hot dog sized ice fragments, dropped from burdened branches and buried in the snow, emerged again like fossils, and we marveled over them and relived the Ice Storm.

Now, six years later, predictions for snow brought out child-like glee in even the adults at school, despite the fact that a vacation day in June is traded each time, but the threat of ice brings a dark, subdued anticipation. Nervous giggles. People without wood stoves or generators, whose roofs are covered with too much snow, have hearts etched with worry.

I called David an hour after he left, and the roads were fine for the slow drive into town. The layer of snow the road crew left had done its job absorbing the sleet, and the truck went through it without a problem. Virtually no one else was on the road, and he'd already heard that he'd be heading back home early, well before dark.

Kodiak curled up at my feet, and the power didn't even flicker. Ice storms are nature's natural tools for pruning, and our power lines have been pretty clear for about six years. The sleet didn't let up much, but the chickadees still made mad dashes to the feeders from the sheltering firs. We heard that branches and treetops, the most nutritious parts, were so accessible to the animals after the Ice Storm that both birds and their four-footed counterparts foraged well. Nature's silver lining.

Splitting Cane

"He needs six splits of cane for each tip, and a spare or two would be nice, just in case."

During the second week of February, the temperature suddenly dropped, and the snowshoe trail was a float frozen so solid that snowshoes were no longer necessary. The days were a tiny bit longer, though. The sun hadn't quite set before it was time to head out on our evening hike with Kodiak. David was occupied with unpacking a newly arrived form for planing cane, so I motioned Kodiak toward the north house, and we went up the trail first. David would need a few minutes to inspect the delivery; then he'd gather a few tools and drive over. Empty, open, and spacious, the north house was turning into a great place to work and made a good antidote to cabin fever. With any luck Kodiak and I could make it to the outlet stream and back to rendezvous in front of the warm fire before he'd progressed too far with the cane.

The thermometer read nine degrees. I picked up the pace to get some warmth in my fingers. Besides abandoning the snowshoes, I had exchanged the ice axe I'd carried for weeks for a ski pole. It helped with balance on the float, and I could plant it in the deep snow for rescues. I couldn't get to the ice with the axe if I tried. David and I had been crossing a snowy marsh the day

135

before when my footing gave way over. My boots and gore-tex pants kept me dry in the shallow water, but scrambling out of the pond with snowshoes on, then wallowing through deep snow back to the float, would have been far more difficult without David to lend a hand.

Kodiak was sticking to the float to avoid the deep snow, now over his chest. He'd have to leap to pound his feet to the bottom or swim through it to get anywhere, apparently too much work at the moment. He'd run ahead, come back, look past me at the return trail, give up when I didn't turn back, and run ahead again to warm up. The clouds lit up as the sun dropped below them, just at the horizon, before it slipped from sight. With any luck, the clouds would stick around and keep the temperature from dropping much farther.

We had passed the north house, headed down into the marsh, circled to the north end of the pond, and arrived at the stream before I needed my headlamp. There was a dusting of fresh snow on the shelf ice. Fresh tracks made perfect imprints, little tracks an inch across. Five toes, ten-inch stride, overlapping straddle. I would have liked to venture out to inspect them, but I was feeling cautious. There hadn't been any shelf ice two days before. Plus, Kodiak was still asking to go back. I radioed David that he was on his way and turned around.

David had a welcoming fire going in the Jotel and had set up a portable workbench in the vacant living room. My little school desk, a useful discard from an elementary school, was set up on the opposite side of the fire. Kodiak's bed was in between. The three of us had plenty of room to work (or sleep) and keep out of each other's way. That was the theory, any way. Kodiak spent most his of time whining.

The workbench was the portable counterpart of the one next door. David clamped on a small vise and then locked a potato knife in its jaws. The knife lay at an angle, handle down and braced on the bench, the blade extending a couple of inches above the vise at about a forty-five degree angle. A culm of cane, hand fed against the blade, would be forced down as it split. This was a method we'd learned at the Canadian rod makers' gathering, Canadian Cane, last May.

Over Memorial Day weekend, we'd left Kodes to visit with his Aunt Barb and drove east, past Lake Ontario, to the little village of Elora to meet our Michigan friends, Janet and Coh and their girls. We shared a bed and breakfast and the hospitality of a German farmhouse nicer than any farmhouse I'd ever seen. Coh, David, and I joined old friends, some only virtual acquaintances who now had faces to go with their names. Ron Barch met us at the car, and I could see Carole Medved with Clara the Dog through the pavilion door. Jorge Carcaro had once advised David on ferrule repair by e-mail; it was nice to shake his hand. The program of demonstrations and activities was organized by Ted Knott, Mark Babiy, and others, and the rain moving in only meant that we'd all be gathered in the pavilion and have to forego casting rods until there was a break in both the clouds and the conversation.

John Long had orchestrated the Grand Experiment, named in part for the nearby Grand River, an idea spawned in these waters at the last gathering. Makers from across two countries had created rods based on the same taper but incorporating a variety of differences, flamed or not, impregnated, nodeless, hexes, quads, pentas, heat-treated or not, and more. They were outfitted with nearly identical components, reels, and lines. Comment sheets were available at the casting pool, and phase two was to begin;

which rods cast better? A grand experiment, but a bit dampened by the rain.

There was plenty more to keep us occupied. Tom Smithwick demonstrated straightening cane with an alcohol lamp and brushing on varnish as an alternative to dipping, dripping, or spraying. We covered such details as choosing an ink that would write well on bamboo; the British, it seemed, spiral their signatures, whereas North Americans tend to write along a facet or two. Side conversations emerged about taper details, Olaf Borge's silk lines, sources for pit-free cork, and, as usual, good fishing and good food. John Zimny showed us square ferrules for quads, and Al Medved demonstrated rattan grips. I was overwhelmed with the level of support in the room, an incredible group of people. We were honored to meet Jon Bokstrom, and Ron Grantham demonstrated Jon's paring knife method of splitting culm-length cane into fine, even strips. And he did it bare handed, to the good-natured wincing of the experienced observers.

The two culms of cane David had flamed over the weekend, scorching them slightly to a beautiful, rich brown, were going to be transformed into a F.E. Thomas 7'6" 3 piece four-weight rod, bound for Colorado. Delivery was to be approximately in July. Its eventual owner had supplied the taper and his own reel seat. He seemed like a great guy, and David was happy to be making a rod for him. David likes the idea of holding the price of a bamboo rod within the reach of anyone who appreciates them.

Up until the Grand Gathering, David split strips of cane from the culm by pounding a nail through a node in the bamboo and pulling the resulting splits past it. By splitting the bamboo instead of cutting it, the theory goes, there is less danger of slicing through a power fiber, the sinuous thread that runs the length of the cane and gives it strength. Split strips should run fairly straight, following the natural grain of sorts of the bamboo. If a split wanders one way or the other, adjusting the angle of the pull, or maybe the amount of force, might direct it back into line. After a few culms, one begins to believe that there must be a better way. David tried forcing a knife through the cane and toyed with the idea of buying a star shaped splitter. The Canadian method seemed worth a try.

To prepare for splitting the bamboo intended for the Colorado rod, David had filed the enamel of the nodes down a bit after flaming the cane by scorching it with a torch throughout its length. The flaming may or may not provide a heat treating advantage, but it does give a nice antique brown look. He matched the nodes to allow for the proper spacing for this rod and cut the culms to length. He was about to make the first split when we both abandoned any thought of concentrating. Kodiak was driving us nuts. He had everything a dog could want and still he kept it up. Usually, he wants something when he talks, almost like a Siamese cat, and we get the point, but this time we didn't have a clue. We tried to ignore him and finally couldn't stand it.

"What do you want?" we asked again, exasperated. He wasn't telling. David tried a distraction.

"Let's go downstairs and get some wood," he offered. Kodiak led the way, and then I heard David yell something about coming and looking to see and then saying something to Kodiak about a mouse. He came up the stairs with a soggy but breathing vole suspended from his fingers by the ruff of its neck.

"Kodes found him," he said, somewhat proudly I thought.

The lengths of cane each had a drying split already, so David decided to divide them at that split before measuring for the rest.

He put on his gloves, held the cane horizontally against the secured knife blade, and tapped the butt with a rubber hammer to get the split started. The cane replied with a crack, and he pushed the culm ahead, the split rushing to the first node. A quick twist and the split cracked through the node and ran on.

Once the length of the cane split into two pieces, David removed as much of the dams formed in the interior of the culm by the nodes as he could easily using a fan-shaped gouge. Then he measured the pieces of cane to see how many splits he could safely make out of each one, and marked them with a felt marker in two or three places along each length. He needs six splits of cane for each tip, and a spare or two would be nice, just in case. If he could get twelve splits from a section, he'd have just enough for two matched tips. Fourteen would mean emergency spares. Eighteen, and the mid could be matched, too. Twenty-four, the butt.

I worked across the room, keeping an eye on his progress. Kodiak was finally back on his bed, only slightly satisfied with apprehending the intruder, and it was growing obvious that he wanted to go home to bed. Eight o'clock, every night. Dog of habit. If we won't go upstairs, he'll eventually go without us, providing we're at the right house.

David aligned the blade with the first section's marker lines, and tapped the end of the cane. The blade bit into the end of the culm and cracked through, a perfect split. The second split was a bit more reluctant, but a tiny bit of pressure on the stick in the direction it was wandering from the marks put it right back on course. This sure seemed to beat the nail-through-the-node splitting method. He repeated the process a few more times, then looked up and grinned.

"This is working too well," he smiled, and paused to let restless Kodiak outside. "If we don't come out, are you gonna raise some hell?" he asked.

Kodiak waited while David tied the little nylon line that fools Kodiak into thinking he's tethered to the D-ring in his collar with a quick release knot. When David opened the door, Kodiak bounded out indignantly to the end of his line. He stood there, back to us, surveying the dark night.

David closed the door against the cold and picked up the last of the cane to mark. It's hard to concentrate when you know what's going to happen next. We looked down, me at the laptop, David at the next section of cane. Nothing yet. I tried to start typing; David placed the cane on the vise and tapped the butt. Crack, then splitting sounds. Then finally Kodiak, testing the night for any neighbor dog within earshot. I laughed; he was almost on cue. Past 8 o'clock, Kodiak will resort to almost anything to distract us and get his way. The barking escalated. If he were a wolf, there'd been a pack called in. David split one more strip, and we gave up. Thanks to Jon, Ron, and a host of others, there had been enough progress for one night, and we could take Kodiak home to bed. I leashed him for the quick walk by starlight, and David tossed the extra gear into the car.

Multitudes of squirrels and snowshoe hares had been thumping across the trail to the south house since we'd left. Their tracks were everywhere in the fresh snow. A taunting dog torture, which fell on our deaf ears. How can Kodiak be expected to protect his territory with such riff-raff about? He marked and re-marked all of his spots while I tried to visualize the gentle creatures' activity which must have been taking place all evening in the dark, secretly, except to Kodiak. David easily beat us home. He went in to start the fire.

We ducked through the canoe shed and rounded the house into the clearing, dwarfed under a spectacular scene. The clouds had dissipated, and the temperature was dropping after all, but the view was worth it. Orion the Hunter stretched from nearly horizon to zenith in the southern sky. His bow was tipped with a brilliant arrow, aimed at the Pleiades, the wild geese, a cluster of stars always just beyond reach. The stars of his knife were suspended by the three stars of his belt, where the nebula hides. At his heels trailed the Dog Star, and, just over his shoulder, the planet Jupiter glowed gigantic. To the northwest, the W that is Cassopeia, and, to the northeast, the Big Dipper, the front stars of its bowl pointing to the North Star, roughly nine fists high above the horizon, about forty-five degrees. It was breathtaking. Who could ever be afraid of the dark?

The Mink

*"We could see it there,
watching us watch it."*

W e weren't supposed to be heading home. Two days of
February vacation had been stolen away by storms in the Midwest.
We had had to leave for the Portland Jetport before 4 a.m. if we
were to catch our flight. A lull in the snowstorm that had blown
in was predicted, a forecast that we were glad to see was accurate.
We had shared the road south with snowplows and newspaper
carriers, just the right amount of traffic to keep us company and to
remind us where the edge of the road should be. We were in line
with the other early but already weary-eyed travelers who'd braved
the snow-covered roads when we heard: no planes had come into
the jetport the previous night from the hub in Cleveland - there
were none to go back out.

It could have been pretty discouraging. School vacation
flights are always overbooked, and the best we could wrangle was a
two-day delay. We love winter, though, so our perspectives may
have been different from the other frustrated Florida travelers.
Our first weekend wasn't stolen; it was a gift. Two free days at
home in the woods of Maine in winter.

The lull passed, and the storm intensified before we finished the seventy mile crawl back north. We broke through the plow's drift at the end of the driveway around noon and weighed the merits of clearing the snow twice in one day against taking a nap until the blizzard was over. Kodiak hopped on to the foot of our bed, never realizing how close he'd come to a full week with his dog-cousin, and it was decided. Naps.

The snow was light and fluffy, and we enjoyed the low sunlight of the late afternoon. David took the snowblower out to tackle the drifts the plow had mixed liberally with gravel, adding to the challenge by constantly threatening to sheer impeller or auger pins. I shoveled the decks, the door landings, and the paths to the basement windows while Kodiak supervised; then we went out to the canoe shed and freed the snow from the roof. It piled on the ground high enough to reach the eaves.

The afternoon was warm enough for shirtsleeves, hat, and mittens, but the clear night would mean plummeting temperatures. Kodiak inspected the woodpile for mice while I loaded birch on toboggans for a ride to the basement door. When David finished, he parked the snowblower on a southeast facing slope for a good thawing the next day and helped me pile the wood inside.

The moon rose slowly, orange and full, over towering pines instead of palms, but we were warm watching it together, surveying our peaceful clearing and enjoying a perfect night. There wasn't a sound. The ice that speaks all night as it freezes in November and December was silenced by a foot of new powder, over two feet of accumulation. Balsam firs and hemlocks were so still that they hadn't lost a flake all day; by moonlight we could see that they wore beautiful blankets of white. No wind, no snowmobiles, no one braving the marginal road. The night was so precious it could have been the special moment in anyone's vacation.

The sun was unusually warm the next morning, and the temperature rose into the twenties by early afternoon. David stayed behind to prepare the snowblower for future use, and Kodiak and I snowshoed out to repack the float. He ran ahead to the area of the grass covered, and now snow covered, south beaver dam while I tried to lay an even track. Something had been up at the Grass Dam; the Kodes had been digging down to it through the snowpack for three days like a dog obsessed. We'd try to entice him on to Bull Moose Cove, but he couldn't be distracted. Even if I leashed him and led him a quarter of a mile, he would sit obediently while I freed him but then tear back to the Grass Dam. By the time I'd snowshoe back, he'd be a rooster tail of flying snow, pausing just long enough to look up, grinning through a snow-covered face, re-adjust his position, and have at it again. We were mystified.

It was different this time when we reached the Grass Dam. He wasn't interested at all. I packed the trail across the dam, up the sparkling hill to the hemlocks, across the ridge, and down to Bull Moose Cove. Dramatic black clouds broke from the west just as we headed on to the ice and started back south. Near white-out conditions. I radioed David in amazement; I could hardly even see our clearing on the opposite side of the pond. But before I could tell him, the snow stopped. Winter is so cool.

Kodiak was oblivious. There were very fresh tracks extending east from the beaver lodge turned igloo, and he was intent on following them across the ice. Unfortunately, they didn't parallel the snowshoe float, so he had to leap to clear enough snow to move forward, porpoising away from me. We both decided it was far too much effort at the same time. I called; he came.

Kodiak led as we broke a new trail off the Big Pond and retraced the float to the Grass Dam. We were both tired. Kodiak trotted on ahead toward the cutoff to the Big Rock Point, and his played out mine of old digging holes, just below our clearing. In case he found his way up and out the driveway, I radioed David to step outside for the interception, and I veered off to the Big Rock to see if he was digging at the snow covered shoreline.

David and I both heard the screech. It sounded like a prehistoric raptor. Oh, no, I thought, has Kodiak wounded an eagle? Then we heard the yipe. Oh, no, I thought, an eagle has wounded Kodiak. One had snatched a dachshund on the Kennebec already, and the incident must have been on my mind. Admittedly, Kodiak was fifty pounds heavier, and the little dog did get away. I really had no idea what to expect. David was radioing from the top of the hill, and I was struggling to break a new trail to the pond.

"I can't see him yet!" I yelled into the handset. "Come down and help me!"

I broke out of the firs on to the ice and saw Kodiak barking at a wood duck nesting box. As soon as he saw me, he lay down like a sphinx, wild eyes trained on the hole, grinning from ear to ear. David radioed. He was mired to his waist in snow and not making much time. With no apparent danger to Kodiak imminent, he retreated to put on snowshoes while I labored up the pond to Kodiak, who was happy to see me. There wasn't a sound from the box.

Minutes later, David arrived with a flashlight. With the squalls over, the snow-reflected sunlight was so brilliant that the beam was lost, even shining into the box. We couldn't see down into the bottom, anyway, because of the angle of the hole. David and I were both a little nervous. Kodiak was adamant, even though there was still no sound from the box.

What to do?

Maybe there was nothing there. Kodiak can be fooled. I tested the darkness with the end of my ski pole. Something hissed. We didn't want to terrorize a poor, entrapped animal. Since Kodiak was convincing us it was a cat, which would make a dog the probable source of the greatest stress, we finally decided to take him home and bring back a screwdriver to open the box. Kodiak wasn't happy.

How exactly does one extract an unknown animal from a duck box? We weren't even sure it would still be there after the time it took us to follow David's new float to the house and back. Faint old tracks came and went; it had been in the box and moved on before. The closest part of the pond to the house, and we hadn't been in the area all winter. We found tracks near the Big Rock which told the story of Kodiak overtaking it, scuffling, and then following it to the box. The snow was too deep to distinguish the prints.

We talked it over. David would stand in back of the box and remove the doorscrew. I would keep an eye on the hole in front from a few feet away. As soon as he started working, a face peeked out and then leaned around to watch him work on the screw, a luxurious, deep brown face with a white chin. David freed the screw and hit the door to loosen the ice's hold on it. The mink retreated, and I could smell the odor from ten feet away.

While we'd never actually seen one, we've known that there could be mink in the area. Shored up by beaver engineered dams, the chain of ponds is a clear soup of dace, turtles, frogs, and another delight of mink dietary preferences, muskrats. Mink have a reputation for a nasty personality; neither of us was sure what a mink in a wood duck box would do. We regrouped in the bright sunlight on the still sparkling snow, staring into each other's sunglasses. We were warm, happy, and still a little nervous. A mink in the duck box!

We needed to clean all of the boxes before March, when meltwater on top of the ice makes for slushy snowshoeing. All eleven boxes get used every year, mostly by wood ducks but occasionally by merganzers. We keep a detailed chart of their use, and I vaguely remembered that this one generally contains a few second-clutch eggs left behind to freeze solid. With several inches of wood shavings and duck down, a potentially fully stocked pantry, and still enough height above the snow to deter canids yet be within leaping distance, this mink had hit the jackpot.

But Kodiak now knew where he was. We could envision that same obsessive behavior that gave us three days of digging at the Grass Dam, the southern terminus of the mink tracks, directed at this wood duck box. The mink would have to move on for its own sake and for peace in our family.

I stepped back, thinking of the camera packed away in our luggage. David pried the side door flap open with the screwdriver, and the mink leaned out the front hole and watched. He was big enough to completely fill the opening; his girth was about the same as a wood duck's, much bigger than I had imagined. I guess I've seen too many ermine. The richness of his fur was stunning. The sunlight played, making highlights and shining waves as he moved to get a better view.

Still, he didn't move very far. He seemed quite curious about us and quite unafraid as he looked us over, half in, half out of the box. To resolve the deadlock, David reached in through the side door and gave him a slight touch with the handle of his ski pole. The mink hissed at the indignity and jumped down. We were relieved to see that he was all right; there weren't even wet mouthing marks on his fur from Kodiak, so their encounter must have been brief.

The mink casually leaped toward the shore, showing off that fatal coat in the sunlight and disappearing into the soft powder, again and again, until it reached an old log. It slipped underneath, but we could see it there, watching us watch it. Make yourself at home; sorry about the intrusion.

That evening, the moon was cold and bright and full again, and we wished the mink good hunting. It would be easy to see its prey in the moonlight, easy for its prey to see harm approach. Probably it would have to hunt under the snow, maybe tunnel near the beaver stick and grass homes of the mice on the back side of the Grass Dam.

Kodiak lay in the flickering light and cozy warmth of the woodstove, staring through the glass doors at the flames. Probably remembering his own indignity of the day, he occasionally licked the top of his right paw, the paw he uses to swat toys when we play or might use to test a mink overtaken on the way to its condo. We sat on the thick dog bed on either side of him and enjoyed the fire together. I had thought the moonlight with its silence after the storm was our gift for the vacation delay. Sometimes, things only get better.

Redfish

"It seems like most of Maine has relatives in Florida or maybe just the urge to feel warm again."

Anyone traveling south over February school vacation from Maine gets used to long lines in airports and the potential for getting bumped from flights. It seems like most of Maine has relatives in Florida, or maybe just the urge to see daylight and feel warm again. The two of us are reluctant snowbirds, and we often tell my mom and stepdad that it would be easier and more fun to visit them if they lived somewhere north and cold. They smile as if we'll change our tune someday, and we join the crowd headed south for one week every year.

With so much of Maine's small population on the move, it's not unusual to run into someone you know, even after a two-day delay, even as far away as the airport in Atlanta. Still, we were a bit surprised to hear our names called from the shoe-shine booth. Our footwear is usually a variant of sneakers or hiking boots. It seemed a little surreal knowing someone getting his shoes shined on the way to Florida.

"Hey, are you guys in a hurry? I need to talk to you!" Not quite the greeting we expected, either. "I really want a bamboo fly rod, and I was thinking I'd like to order one from someone I know,

but I don't really know how to do it? What do you need to know?"
We smiled back at the sheepish and sincere face of the high school
principal, Jim Marascio.

The real advantage of a split cane fly rod is also its most bewil-
dering attribute: too many choices. We talked briefly, there in the
Atlanta airport. David asked questions like 'where do you usually
fish?' and 'what do you usually fish for?'. Lengths and line weights
just touch the surface: taper selection relates to the action desired;
components determine aesthetics (which are pretty important for
rod-gazing through long Maine winters). They decided to get
together in the next few weeks and that David might be able to
finish the rod by the next December; Jim was in no hurry. Minutes
later, we were on our plane and whisked into the air.

I'm especially lucky as these things go; as a result of the
divorce that separated two parents I dearly love, I have four parents
I love and hold dear. My Florida parents, Mom and Archie, are
perfect hosts. We're all totally comfortable together and we enjoy
each other's company, but we're also perfectly comfortable apart.
They're not fly anglers, but they are one hundred per cent
supportive, so, as usual, we were greeted with warm hugs, a pile of
newspaper clippings of fishing reports, and a handful of helpful
maps. They had even scouted a few locations, including a nearby
interior lake where male alligators bellowed in November and
locals still tempt bass in the channel with traditional cane poles. I
helped Mom and Arch pick the grapefruit from the loaded tree in
their yard while David climbed the ladder for a little carport
maintenance. Mom happily indulged us in a trip to Lehr's Tackle
for the best fly fishing scoop and was just as happy that we had
something to do on the evenings she bowls or in the early
mornings when their little neighborhood is still sleepy.

There's an undeveloped beach ten minutes away lined with mangroves and in reach of enough sea grass within wading distance to be promising. The first day, the tides were with us for early morning angling in clear, out going water. Brown pelicans were making neck-breaking dives just offshore. We appreciated the tip and tied on small clouser minnows to imitate the real minnows they must have been after. We waded to thigh deep and cast into that range, wary of being too close and enticing a bird. There was no one on the beach. The sand was white and powder fine and dotted with the little wet sandmounds sea worms make when they burrow. Their discarded protective lairs, like those of caddis larva, were near each one.

Other animals were having more success than we were. Ospreys flew by, just barely gaining enough elevation to clear the mangroves, a chubby fish always clenched face-forward in their right talons. The pelicans were so friendly that they started fishing between us; in the still morning air, we could hear the clatter of their beaks as they ate their catches.

We worked our way down the sand toward a small canal that came out of the mangroves. My wrist was aching already from casting. Fishing the surf is work compared to casting dry flies with my bamboo rod. The canal cut a fifteen foot wide path through the beach, and I knelt to see if it was shallow enough for wading. Probably. Then David called out an alert.

"Dolphin!"

I looked up at a bottlenose, a flipper clone, not twenty feet up the canal and headed my way. David appeared beside me. We heard it breathe, looked into its eyes, and watched the wake as it cruised past. Another fisherman.

Cast, strip in. Cast, strip in. It's great to be outside, but this sure wasn't sight fishing. I was more interested in the wading birds, I'll admit. We have a great blue heron rookery in our big pond, and the southern cousins were stalking their prey nearby. These are sight fishermen, and pretty successful ones, too. A white morph was wading, distinguishable from the ibis by a straight, yellow bill as opposed to a curving orange one and by the hunting style. An ibis pokes around in the sand just under the water, feeling for food as opposed to snatching little fish. Little blue herons are half the size of the Great Blues and have a blue-black head and bill. They're little stalking predators and remind me of pint-sized Jurassic raptors. Snowy egrets are roughly the same size but are white like the much larger ibis and the white morph of the great blue heron. Snowys have mostly black bills, but their legs and feet are the real give-away; black legs with yellow feet make them look like they stepped into paint somewhere. Their head feathers can be extended into long, regal plumes. These little guys come to the coastal Maine marshes. Similar in size, white cattle egrets are more likely found on the lawns or in pastures than on the beach. They look relatively small, streamlined, and plain, but are experts at crossing traffic. They are also experts at deftly snatching flies off the side of my dad's garage in Michigan, a rare summer event. Those bills never touch the siding.

I was watching the LBB's, the little brown birds, mining the shoreline and scampering to avoid waves as if they were controlled by a single mind when my retrieve felt different. Must have caught something.

"Got a fish!" I told myself and David. It wasn't fighting much, but it was definitely something. I brought it closer.

"What is it?" David called back, stripping in. "Should I come over?"

I looked down into two green eyes (I could see both of them on the front), a maze of stripes, and little horns. A psychedelic bullhead?

"Pooh," said the little porcupine fish, shooting a column of water out of its mouth. "Pooh, pooh."

I was a bit taken back but not offended. It was put out, but it was still polite.

"I'll walk him over to you," I called back and led my fish like a puppy in David's direction, taking care to keep it in clear water. It seemed like a very sturdy little fish. David had the extra long needle nosed pliers. I wasn't entirely sure we should even touch the fish; it had skin instead of scales, and I took its coloration as a fair warning. I'm not sure if he took the clouser minnow or if I just snagged him in the corner of his mouth, but he was perfectly willing to hang out with us once he was released. Friendly little fish, to be sure.

We headed back, stopping only to rescue a stranded horseshoe crab. It's always hard to know when to interfere. Maybe the crab chose to be on shore for some instinctual reason, but there were a few skeletons on the beach, and sentimentality got the better of me. As an attempt at compromise, we left him just barely in the water, an easy place to climb out again or to return to the Gulf.

We set out the next morning in a canoe with the knowledge that I, at least, wouldn't be skunked this trip, but David still offered to let me take the first turn casting from the bow. Our technique is to rent a seventeen foot Old Town canoe from the Tarpon Bay concession on Sanibel Island, a short distance from Mom and Archie's place. We use the little electric trolling motor to speed to the far end of the bay, pausing to admire birds or dolphins, or to avoid sandbars, and then fish just off the mangroves. One of us paddles quietly; the other stands and casts. We both keep an eye peeled for fish.

Last year, David was casting when I spotted a big redfish. He dropped a fly just in front of it, and everything fell into place. The fish took the clouser minnow and ran toward the mangrove roots, but David played him back while I positioned the canoe so that the red wouldn't run underneath. When it turned and ran toward deeper water, we decided that it might be a little bigger than we thought. The redfish started pulling the canoe. I knew this was going to be one of those times when I would be glad that David was playing the fish.

He didn't want the fish to be too tired to release, and the red must have agreed because it came back. I had the sudden realization that a greater responsibility was on my shoulders. The proof of this whole event lay in my hands. Where was that camera, anyway? I freed it from the dry bag and tried to get a shot. David was leaning over the gunwhale in the way.

"Lift him into the boat," I said, a bit too excited to say it politely. David paused in his struggle and looked at me.

"I'm trying."

"Oh."

Then we were both laughing. This was a heavy fish for trout anglers, and a canoe isn't the most stable platform in the world. I started snapping pictures, just in case the worse happened, and shot a nice sequence of red drum wrestling. This, too, is a durable fish.

David rolled the red on to his lap and compared it to the yardstick painted on the inside of the canoe. Longer than that. We tried two legitimate poses and then lowered the fish, free of the fly, back into the bay. He wasn't very friendly and swam right off.

I hoped for an encore this trip. The wind had come up before my turn to try last year, and we had headed directly back to the dock. Despite my bow seat and David's best encouragement, this year my arm gave out before the fish gave in. We switched seats, and he cast down the west side of the bay. At one point we saw snook; at one point we saw six frantic reds escaping something that had spooked them before they saw us. The windspeed slowly climbed, and we knew it was over.

At the airport we were still discussing those fleeing reds and wishing we knew more about them. The place was packed from overbooked flights and another crowd of already disheartened passengers headed north, or so they hoped. Business as usual on these school vacation weekends. We didn't mind. We have learned a little about the habits of airlines, which, like fishing, occasionally work out for the best. As soon as our gate opened, we offered to delay our travel if tickets on our flight were needed. It feels like risky business, and nothing is certain until the proof is in hand, also like fishing, but that night we were only four hours late arriving home, and we were two free airline tickets richer. We'll read up on redfish before we use them.

LATE WINTER

Just then I saw a

young hawk flyin',

and my soul

began to rise.

Bob Seger

Faux Snowmelt

"The last gasp efforts of a winter nearly over."

March came in right after we returned from Florida, regardless of what the calendar said. March, the month of almost daily change. The month when temperatures rise to almost fifty and the sky is summer-blue only to be followed by sub-zero nights and howling winds, the last gasp efforts of a winter nearly over. Every slight variance makes a difference in the weather and in people's attitudes. David and I watch both, sort of an end-of-the-winter pasttime.

Forty degrees and sun, and most people smile. It's a heat wave with spring right around the corner, imminent, almost close enough to touch. Ground fog that night, but who cares? It's almost spring. Everyone knows that it's not almost spring; the realists will even point out all the past evidence that the snows always return, but a couple of days of persistent sun wins hopeful converts.

Then there's forty degrees with precipitation, plain old rain, and some good-natured philosophy: at least the snow is melting. We can live with this; after all, it's March. At thirty-two degrees the precipitation is freezing rain, bone-chilling dampness, usually enough to provoke a little reactionary contempt. What's with this weather...isn't it March, for Pete's sake?

Drop two more degrees to thirty, add precipitation, say, over a foot of snow, and it's nearly universal PMS (Put-out with March Syndrome). How long is this winter going to last anyway? We don't mess with anyone afflicted. Last April we had two eighteen-inch snowstorms. While there were a few who could take the joke, it wasn't just the wind that was howling. At times every year, usually in March, our road muddies up or washes out with the thaw, and we're temporarily isolated from the fickle world. It's just as well because March is one of our twelve most favorite months.

So even though it was the end of February, it was acting like a March Sunday. The sun was noticeably higher in its arc and felt warmer than the forty degree reading on the thermometer, probably because the sky was such an uninterrupted deep blue that the most devout March grump couldn't help but smile. Warmth from the inside out.

By ten a.m., we'd finished every chore that had to be done and were weighing the situation. David had bamboo strips to straighten, and I had some work ahead on the laptop, but both, we concurred, could wait until dark in front of the woodstove. On the other hand, at forty degrees the snowmobile trails would turn from packed ice to spring snow conditions, and they should be pretty deserted if we chose the right places. Air-cooled snowmobiles might overheat at forty, so at least the numbers would be down. The United States versus Canada Olympic hockey game was on the docket for the afternoon, and that would have some draw, as should the sled dog races and winter carnivals in Farmington and Millinocket. The snow was pretty much gone downstate, so there could be some out-of-sight, out-of-mind effects on the winter recreation enthusiasts. Sun, good trail conditions, end of the season solitude, albeit a bit early: it all added up nicely.

"Want to go cross country skiing?" we asked Kodiak. He always does and was a moving obstacle the entire time we were digging for gear. We decided not to take the time to wax the skate skis; our skinny but high performance waxless would be faster now, to get going, and faster there, if the conditions or our endurance betrayed us. David threaded the long, skate skiing ski poles out of the rafters near the fly rods, though. We'd have no need of bigger baskets for buoyancy on the trails where we were headed. We left a message on his sister's answering machine so someone would know where we'd gone and drove north.

Just beyond Skowhegan and Bingham, following the Upper Kennebec Valley, the roadsides transform into seemingly endless paper company land. The road winds away northward toward Moosehead Lake, but we turned off. One of our favorite trails masquerades as a logging road all summer but transforms into a snowmobile trail when the weather turns. By March, it's a wide packed route leading into the highlands and foothills and farther to Quebec. On the return trip, there are views of the Kennebec Valley and Bigelow and Sugarloaf Mountains beyond. This isn't the sexy, scenic kind of place that gets overrun with people, and there are snowmobile trails with better parking, access to bigger lakes, or linking to bigger towns. What would appear to be only moderately attractive at first glance, therefore, becomes amazing upon further scrutiny, a great trail where the most likely visitors are moose and coyotes, and us.

We walked away from the truck and around the bend still carrying our skis and leashing Kodiak. The clearing right along the road was usually a yarding area for logs or parking for skidders or snowmobilers, but it was too close to traffic to let the Kodes run free. Walking bought us a little time to check out the trail conditions. The surface was springlike, the perfect soft, almost slushy snow, barely coating the firm trail beneath, as long as we were in the sun. In the shade, it turned back to hard, clattery ice. Could be tricky, but with most of the trail bright and luring us on, we were up for anything.

David took off first, double poling long, alternating skates. Zero to gone, just like that. Kodiak ran to pass him when I unsnapped his leash, and I tested a safe diagonal stride until I caught them both at the top of the first grade. The next hill, shady and steep, dropped to a logging bridge.

"You first," I grinned.

David pushed off and clattered into the shade as his skis hit ice. He bent his knees and held a wide stance across the bridge and back into the light, then herringboned up the next hill in the sun, never losing his momentum. My scout through unscathed, I could see no reason for caution. I pushed off, dropped into a deep tuck, and flew down after him, clattering across the ice-coated logging bridge and coasting right up to David's skis.

I felt good.

We pulled off our hats and shared the water bottle. The day was going to be sweet, and we both knew it. It just couldn't be any better. We took off again, both skating as long as our arms held out, then saved by a downhill run, and off again. The skiing was as close to effortless as it gets and the trail so smooth we had time to enjoy the views. The sun reflected off the snow, feeling as intense as Sanibel fishing had five days earlier. Wading Wednesday, skiing Sunday. Flexibility, that's our motto.

We glided around a curve and found two snowmobilers, helmets and gloves off, sled hoods raised, so we stopped to talk. They weren't the least concerned about their situation.

"Hi. Overheat?" David asked, keeping an eye on Kodiak.

"Yeah, it's a little warm," the nearer guy said. Neither was over twenty, and they were quite congenial.

"Is there anything we can do?" I asked.

"Nah, they'll go when they cool off. We don't mind waiting." That seemed to be true. They were perfectly happy out on a sunny Sunday afternoon.

David, meanwhile, was directing Kodiak away from the farther snowmobile. The Kodes hadn't actually lifted his leg, but he looked like he was considering it. Kodiak once marked his possession of the poet laureate of Maine, or, rather, tried to mark a rock he was standing on and hit the more distinguished target instead. We'd been out walking behind our pond and came across our notable neighbor and his wife. We stood and talked for quite awhile, all in snowshoes and all oblivious to the fact that Kodiak's marker stone was buried in the snow somewhere beneath our neighbor's feet. Kodiak was well aware of it and finally couldn't think of any better solution than to sidle up to Maine's honored poet and lift his leg. Fortunately our neighbor was wearing knee high rubber boots and had a patient sense of humor, certain that it wasn't a literary critique. We were fairly mortified.

We wished the snowmobilers good luck and double-poled. The trail had a slight downhill grade and a perfect sun-slushed surface for skating. I love it when I'm skiing in front of someone and conditions conspire to make me look like I know what I'm doing. It doesn't always happen that way. David, of course, looked better. It's harder to have long, graceful strides when you're five feet

165

tall than it is when you're approaching six feet. There are at least ten extra inches of inseam per leg to stretch out and glide. My compensation is that that extra height raises his center of gravity, too, and therefore gives me a stability edge. That, coupled with his quiet but decided tendency to push his limits, makes me inclined to hang back on steep grades. He can sprawl into a formidable obstacle mid-way down a hill.

Not this time, though. We curved out of the sun together, joyously in stride, and dropped down a shady, icy curve. Its chatterbumps had grown to near mogul in size, and it ended with a steeply cambered curve that shot us back into the sun. We were both amazed. Invincible. Unscathed. We were the Titans!

When we had first moved to Maine, we settled far to the north in a small town in the St. John River Valley. French was the primary language, and the Miramichi was closer than the Kennebec. We took a small apartment on the second floor of a tidy white house, and the locals joked about it being a good idea since we'd still be able to get out when the snow piled up. The first flakes fell in October, it was below zero before Christmas, and we celebrated the New Year by buying our first pair of cross country skis. We mastered the three pin bindings and the skinny-ski widths in the driveway, then climbed the banks and headed up the long hill behind the house. The snow was deep, actually reaching nearly to our apartment windows, and we were getting used to sidewalks which were tunnels and to payloaders heaping snow from the town's only main street into dump trucks and hauling it off in the night. Winter Carnival was a weeklong holiday, and the snow sculptures rivaled any we'd ever seen.

It took us forty minutes to slog through the deep snow to the roof of the Valley, high on the ridge behind the house. It took

David about three minutes to rocket down, and I might have caught him, but I lost control, made a spectacular, powder snow crash, and found myself burrowed under the snow. It was a riot, and we were in love with winter. We skied over the long, windswept potato fields and into the woods of northern New Brunswick. There were flocks of snow buntings and curious temperature inversions. C'est magnifique! It was only later that we learned that, in fact, no one could ever remember having had snow so deep.

We skied for about an hour on the snowmobile trail then stopped to share the water bottle and assess Kodiak's condition. He was hot and happy but had run half his limit. He made a good excuse; probably we'd pay for it tomorrow, too. We turned, stepping high with the right foot and rotating out and around until that ski could be set down parallel to the left, but pointed back down the trail. Then the left, lifted high and rotated into place beside it. None of that shuffling around in a circle for the Titans!

The views were better on the way back. We swished along, and the white summit of Sugarloaf, where the Appalachian Trail winds southward, and the long bright ridge that is Mount Abraham dwarfed the hills hiding the Kennebec. A layer of stratus clouds was visible behind the mountains, not wispy cirrus mare's tails predicting a change in eighteen hours or so, but the front edge of a slow moving front. Overcast, maybe warmer at night. Miles away, we were still in carefree, light-footed sun, except when the shady, icy hill ate David, and I had to snowplow down to save myself.

The clouds had rolled completely in by the time Kodiak crawled on to our bed and passed out. We'd been adrenaline- high enough to straighten the bamboo strips and finish some notes, but

Monday morning was looming, and we had to get ready. The weather report was on the television in the background, and we both paused to listen. Monday clouds, warm and dry; Tuesday cloudier and damp; Wednesday sleet; Thursday snow; Friday (as if they can see that far ahead) much colder. And Friday, it would actually be March.

The Morning After Owls

*"If you can get a
natural high then why
not a natural hang over?"*

With my eyes closed I could still tell that David was milling around, but I did my best to ignore him. It was early, and I tried to slip under the covers, invisible. I felt worn out, headachy, cotton-mouthed rotten. A natural hangover. I'd never had an actual hangover, but I was guessing this must be close. If you can get a natural high, why not a natural hangover? Too much of a good thing, too late a night, and too much time outdoors: it seems to add up. We'd been out far beyond my bedtime lurking about the area on a mission, an owl census. Right then I was wondering why owls had to be nocturnal or why David had to be diurnal, especially so early.

It was probably a beautiful day. Sometime after I crawled into bed, I heard the weather front coming. There was a faint roar, growing closer, louder, closer and louder, until it shook the house with sudden mid-March wind and pouring rain. It would take more than that to really wake me up, though. For one thing, I knew it was coming. And growing up with fantastic Midwest thunderstorms and occasional tornadoes develops meteorological nerves of steel. The house shook, but I was dog-tired and didn't care. When we'd heard the forecast the day before, we had decided to finish our owl survey before the big change, even if it took most of the night, even if it had been a long week.

We volunteer, with two hundred and fifty other people we've never met, to work on a census of the owl population. It's a joint project of the Department of Inland Fisheries and Wildlife and the Maine Audubon Society that extends over three winters and should give a picture of the health of the ecosystem. Each set of volunteers, encouraged to work in pairs or better for winter safety, is assigned a route and four specific weeks. The volunteers run the route in advance and choose eight sites along it which are at least a mile apart and tactfully placed. No sense disturbing the neighbors. Recordings of owls are furnished and must be tested for volume by measuring the distance they carry from each personal tape deck, hopefully a quarter of a mile or so. Surveyors must go out during three of the weeks specified but choose the day. The time of the trip is predetermined for each week. Some shifts are 7 to 10, some are 10 to 1, and some are assigned entirely after midnight.

David had worked on cane strips all evening. After walking the back trail with Kodiak, I had joined him, dazed yet from all of those good work ideas that seem to converge into a hectic March crescendo when we heard the weather was up to something. For days it had been forty degrees and sunny, a slow-melting, heart warming, late-winter treat. We had put in long hours indoors but had still noticed the animals were moving a lot. On my walk, three tall healthy deer crossed from the downed sweet treetops of the newly logged area to the warmer West Ridge for the night, and, just at dark, we heard a great horned owl with an attitude hissing its presence. Although we were dragging a bit already, the animals and weather seemed cooperative at the moment and that could change. In fact, change seemed quite likely. No wimps-route for us; why not stay out half the night?

Our first survey had been in early February. We'd been assigned the latest shift, and keeping warm was as big an issue as playing the tape and recording the responses. It was our kind of fun even though it took me a couple of days to recover. For the second survey, it had been forty degrees, a comparative heat wave, and should have felt much easier. We drove north a few miles to our starting point, reset the tripometer on the truck, and drove on another mile to our first site. David turned the ignition key to accessory and readied the tape in the portable deck. We listened for three minutes while I noted the conditions: no wind, forty degrees, faint highway noise. No owls, either.

David played the first selection, a great horned owl call, hoo-hoohooo-hoo, hoo-hoohooo-hoo. It repeated a few times. Then we listened three minutes. Nothing. The barred owl call was next. To us, it sounds like "Who cooks for you? Who cooks for you alllll?". That, or we've been taught to think so. It's a good pneumonic, anyway. No owls. After three more minutes of waiting, we played the saw-whet call, too too too too too. I noted on the tally sheet that we had no response.

At our second stop, we heard voices as our ears adjusted to the night. It sounded like two teenage boys, laughing, maybe working on something in the garage nearby. We played the first call, and listened. They revved up an old snowmobile, switched on its Cyclopean headlight, and drove across the field right through our listening area. They had no idea we were parked on the road in the dark. Hmmmm. What to do? They stopped and stalled the engine on the top of the first hill, a great spot to listen for owls but right in our way. If we called out, we'd probably scare them.

We had notified the sheriff before we left, just in case someone spotted us and found us suspicious. We decided just to play the next owl. "Who cooks for you?" A flashlight snapped on our position.

"Who's that? Who's there?" They seemed a bit nervous.

"Sorry, guys," I called back. "Just doing an owl survey."

"Oh, we're really sorry. Really!" they called back. Nice kids. Then they started the snowmobile and drove it back through our study area. We grinned and moved on.

At the third site, a great horned owl hooted in the distance. At midnight, we heard a saw whet. It was so loud I thought it sounded better than our recording. We continued with our twenty-minute stops and the driving breaks in between where we could talk and keep warm. Drive, listen, play a recording, listen, play another, listen, play another, listen, tally, drive on. Then again. Then again. By the last stop, I was surprised to see a backroom light on in a distant house. I supposed it must be the bedroom. Why weren't these people asleep? Didn't they know how late it was? We played the great horned owl call, and the curtains parted. Someone was silhouetted in the room, craning his head to look up at the trees. In the end, though, it apparently wasn't worth much investigation. The curtains closed and the light went out- too late to look for owls for some people. Smart people. By then, I could have been doing better. I would stand outside to listen while David played the calls and find myself weaving as I literally fell asleep on my feet. I fought the urge until we were done, and David drove us home.

David shuffled closer to my quilt-covered hideout, so I opened one eye. Sun, glaring, so I closed it quickly. He was too polite to ask me to get up, but he knew we'd both regret missing such a great Sunday. What was it? Eight a.m.? The anticipated rain had materialized just before dawn, but the sun had come out to assist the winds in drying things off; patches of grass would be appearing outside as the snow began its retreat. I heard the television news switch to the forecast: sunny, breezy, and thirty-five degrees. I gave in, and dragged myself out of bed. I grabbed a Diet Coke for breakfast, took an aspirin, and grabbed another Coke for the road.

Once we were on our way, it proved to be as great a morning as I'd suspected. Long low rays of late winter sunlight bathed the brown patches emerging in the fields. Shielded from the deepest snowpack by the branches overhanging them, beds of leaves looked warm and inviting on the south sides of the trees, a place to lie back with our heads against the trunks and watch the snow melt. We grabbed some real food in Farmington, then drove on to the west toward Tumbledown Mountain.

The trail we chose starts at an old log-yarding area and winds up the mountain just east of Tumbledown on a logging road turned snowmobile trail, both abandoned during Mud Season, that period between packed snow and dry gravel. It's an in between time we regard as a gift. The fifth season in the North, Mud Season, may be a bit messy, but it imposes a certain level of solitude on places like this. We switched to four-wheel drive to approach the yard and parked the truck on fairly secure ground.

Kodiak bounded up the trail as soon as we unsnapped his leash. I was still moving a little slower than usual but gaining momentum as my head cleared. My attitude was much better, and I still had half a Coke left, so I decided to stash it in an icy freshet for a treat on the way back. David and I were looking for a place to access the stream and safely plant the bottle when we saw a hollow log lying next to the trail, not ten feet away. Sitting peace-fully just inside the near end was a snowshoe hare. A white rabbit, catching some rays in a hollow log. I double-checked that David saw it, too; I didn't think my head hurt enough for hallucinations, but, really, a white rabbit sitting in a hollow log? It hopped off without checking its watch, and I noted that it was neither in a hurry nor completely white. The brown hair underneath was starting to show.

Kodiak, curiously, never saw or smelled the rabbit, but it wasn't the first time we'd seen a snowshoe hare rendered invisible to a predator. When we lived on the far northern border of Maine, the place was so remote we had to drive to Canada to the laundromat, and big brook trout thrived in the stream in the center of town. We had gone off into the North Woods on a similar late winter morning. We parked the truck on a logging road at the point where snow-patched dirt road switched to dirt-patched, snow covered road. We explored the endless woods and had almost returned when a mottled snowshoe hare tore past us, a marten in hot pursuit. We were close enough to see the crest on the marten's chest and to detect a trickle of blood on the rabbit's leg. We thought we were about to witness a life and death struggle and couldn't see how the rabbit had any chance. Then, the hare just dropped to the road. It lay still; we couldn't even see it panting. Brown and white hare, brown and white road. The marten couldn't find it. Whether we had momentarily distracted the marten with our presence so that it glanced away just as the hare stopped, we weren't sure, but it seemed confused. It stopped, too, and looked this way and that and then continued in its previous direction of travel in a nervous hurry, afraid it would go hungry again. As far as I know, it did. The marten ran right past the frozen hare. The snowshoe immediately jumped up and ran back past us and out of sight. We felt a little responsible but couldn't decide if that was a good thing or a bad thing.

The trail we were following on this side of the North Woods started out a little muddy. The road was well drained for a logging trail, but it was frozen underneath, and we had a permafrost effect going on. The first hour switched back and forth between gradual climb and steeper gradient, but it was all up. Tall birches, beech with pale leftover leaves rattling gently in the wind, ash, and other maturing trees guarded the trail from the wind but allowed us to be bathed in sunlight for the climb. We took off our hats and mittens and pulled out our water bottles. Kodiak followed suit, stepping on thin ice to break out a drinking hole in the clear roadside trickle.

Farther up, we saw the large, rectangular holes of a pileated woodpecker. They forage here for carpenter ants, excavating three to six inch cavities, then either impaling the ants on a very long tongue or just dragging the ants back out on its backward-pointing barbs. No one is really sure which. We asked our chickadee expert, ornithologist Herb Wilson, on a walk with science teachers Pam and Ann. We were all studying winter ecology and falling down a lot in an icy college woodlot. He told us that all of the woodpeckers have very long tongues, much longer than woodpecker heads. The pileated's tongue is about five inches long. Instead of curling its tongue in its mouth, a woodpecker retracts its tongue into a sheathed cavity, which wraps over and around the back of its skull and anchors between its eyes. When its tongue is in, it lies over the back of its head and down its forehead. When the tongue darts out, the muscles at the back of the throat slide it forward. I picture those muscles stopping the woodpecker's tongue from shooting completely out like a dart, too.

That was the same walk where we had heard about yellow-bellied sapsuckers, our only woodpecker to migrate south. Sapsuckers make the long horizontal lines of little holes in the willows near our yard. The holes serve as wells, filling with sap, which is very attractive to insects, which are in turn choice fare for the sapsuckers. They only need check the wells and keep them open to maintain a smorgasbord of sap-soaked bugs. The drawback to the method is that trees need to photosynthesize to produce sap, and for that they need leaves. So, from leaf drop until the sap starts flowing again, we're one species of woodpecker short.

The season regressed as we climbed higher. The temperature seemed to drop a little, but it may just have been that the trees were losing their protective height as the wind picked up. As we neared the top of the trail, and the agreed upon time to turn back, staghorn sumac lined the road. In the intense low light, their fuzzy horns stood out a deep, rich red against the still continuous high altitude snow. They were almost as breathtaking on an intimate scale as the view when we turned to descend. Spread out before us was the panorama of the rolling countryside below, the foothills, the stone walls, the fields half free of snow, and Webb Lake, still brilliant white, in the distance. Too early for iceout in the mountains.

The splendor of the scene before us changed only in angle as we descended the trail and back through winter to almost spring. By then, the last remnants of ice on the trail had changed to corn snow, and the footing was more secure. We talked and laughed watching Kodiak bound down the trail ahead of us, disappear around a corner, and reappear as soon as he could master gravity to come back and check on our position. The return trip is always faster, but it's even more so in good company when both your heart and your feet feel light. Up and down, it had been a great workout. In no time at all, I was retrieving my icy cold Coke from the stream.

"How are you feeling?" David asked, as I offered him a toast. I didn't understand what he was asking for a moment, then remembered my slow start.

"Fantastic," I grinned to thank him for setting the day in motion. Apparently the cure for a natural hangover is more of the same.

Signs of spring were infiltrating everywhere we looked on the way home. Maple trees along the road were interconnected by green hoses to white covered buckets, and woodsmoke was rising from outdoor stoves here and there as the sap evaporated into syrup. Just before we reached the main highway, a bluebird flew across the road.

The Last Weekend of Winter

"Nostalgia is funny; sometimes you can feel it coming before the things you love are gone."

George Barnes had been making maple syrup near his shop sometime before we arrived on Saturday. We believe that George could make anything. His fine bamboo rods are a given, and have been since we were kids, but he's an inventive Maine Yankee in the best sense of the word with humor and talent to match. He's been in Harpswell for quite some time, and his father and the fathers before him. In his basement there's a musket an elder Barnes took from the hands of a British spy on an island just off Barnes Point.

Sometime during the week, we'd received word that things were a go for an afternoon rendezvous. The weather turned colder and misty at our end, so we made our way carefully on black ice to the coast. On the rocky peninsula, the roads were clear and the sun was coming out. March in Maine. Jane Barnes was treating us all to lunch, and we munched on George's homemade cheeses while we waited for everyone to arrive. George really can make anything.

Rodmakers' gatherings are usually the stuff of summer, but we felt lucky to be rushing the season a bit. It was the last weekend of winter, but good people laughing over a good table, filling the air with good conversation, is as heartwarming as the lengthening

179

days. We shared news of the winter: the fly fishing shows, places we hoped to fish in the summer, kids, dogs, and the recipe for pickled herring. Before we left the table, George brought out a combination rod made by his old friend Cecil Piece. It was a hex, six-strip construction, but each strip was a laminated sandwich of bamboo and graphite, power fibers and carbon fibers. A spare strip was included in the rod sack, and we admired the detail. Another amazing bit of Yankee engineering by a friend gone by.

We talked a little about the Harpswell rodmakers' gathering, an October event George has arranged. There have been offers to move the gathering north and south, if the time has come to pass the torch. Certainly George had contributed his share, but we all were hoping that we'd be back in Harpswell come fall.

We had an offer to join a summer trip that was still on our minds when we went for a walk the next day. We decided to think it over while hiking into the working forest, timber company land normally busy with skidders and fully loaded logging trucks. Those roads were always deserted during mud season, and Kodiak could romp without bothering anyone or risking an accident. We could check on the progression of the season farther north, and, as an ulterior motive, we could monitor the logging operation hidden far from the view of the road. We hadn't gone that far when we were cross country skiing.

There was just enough snow left on the surface of the dirt road to suspend us above the mud on the sunny stretches and to rob us of any traction on those shady, icy, and, usually, steep downhill stretches, but there was no denying that spring was coming. The snow had retreated along the roadsides, leaving boreal mosses, wintergreen, and reindeer lichen exposed. Large boulders mixed with remnant snowbanks under the cedars and hemlocks, and, in places, the granite of the Canadian Shield arched its back above the ground. Buds were swelling, and some had been nipped off by moose or deer. It seems ironic that the oils that act as antifreeze to protect these early buds also make them highly nutritious for animals hungry at the end of winter. David picked a sapsickle from a little maple overhanging the road, and we took an inventory of the time remaining until summer and all of the things we'd like to do.

We still hadn't been down to further explore Boston. We say that we'll go every year, once we run out of other things to do, probably during mud season. We've been to the science museum and the airport, and I went to a musical and a parade with my principal Jenny and our students once. It looks like an interesting city, but Boston would have to wait for another year.

We'd hoped to get more work done on the north house, maybe transform it into our new home, but it had evolved into a spacious shop and studio in the meantime, plus we had the benefit of discovering its habits in winter. That would be useful as we planned our renovations; we laughed. Justification, true, but two people can't do everything, and we hadn't been idle. The place was thoroughly cleaned, the new hearth and woodstove were broken in, and the wood cookstove had been tested. We'd also cleared winding new trails for hours and looked forward to clearing more as soon as the snow melted. Housework versus trailwork; there's no contest.

Wood. We hadn't used more than a cord in either woodstove and actually hadn't used much other fuel, either. Warm winters mean less time at the woodpile, but we'd still need to supplement our supply. It's nice to be two years ahead.

Wood duck nesting boxes. We'd removed several in the fall, cleaned them thoroughly, and devised extensions to raise them farther above the water. As soon as the ice allowed, we'd go out and remount them. The canoe was already waiting at the water's edge. Along the line of bird boxes, we had already cleaned out those intended for bluebirds although occasionally frequented by chickadees and tree swallows, and they were really for the first broods.

We wandered through our list until we came to the stream, about an hour from our truck. Not much bigger than a trickle, it's bridged by a traditional array of criss-crossed timbers, logging style. We leaned over the edge on our stomachs to survey the water below. It was gin-clear and dancing. We could make out the details of every pebble on the bottom. Lying there in the sunlight, we looked for caddis cases and the tiny beginnings of water cress. The round, white feet of splashwater ice, water which started to drip off low-hanging alder branches but re-froze flat, were still attached to the branch just above the surface of the stream, and hopped and skipped on the burbling water. Hair-capped and club mosses lined the little banks in and among the rocks. Hemlock and cedar made a canopy overhead which encircled the serpentine brook and beaver pond upstream.

Roughly fifty feet from the water's edge, there was a clearcut, or nearly so. Two or three large isolated pines were left standing over the hundred acre cut, sparing it the 'clearcut' title. We wandered up the logging road to look it over. Large piles of slash had been gathered, probably to add to the ease of replanting, but there were no visible ruts or washouts we could see. The stream had certainly seemed up to its usual clarity. Still, the snow which persisted beneath the other trees was melted away where these trees once stood, and the ground must have been much warmer for the direct sunlight.

While it is initially shocking to find one's stomping ground suddenly denuded, the point is driven home that it's not our land. Maine has historically enjoyed a peaceful co-existence between its local timber companies, families who live here and hope to sustain the forest forever, and recreational interests. With the new wave of selling and buying, out of state and even out of country, there are hard questions and even harder decisions ahead. Will far-removed paper companies continue to look to the future and safeguard multiple use, or will they strip and sell, allowing wild lakes to become developed and logging roads to acquire gates? There's talk of a new North Woods Park, a chance to protect what's left and balance multiple uses, but such talk makes traditional Mainers, unused to public lands, nervous.

It deserves hours of thought and hours of talk, and we've given it both, but today was not the day. Nothing had changed, for better or worse, since the last time we had been at this spot, except that it was almost spring. Kodiak had waited long enough for the signal to tear back, and we gave the word.

A summer trip north had been proposed, far north in Quebec. The place seemed like Shangri-la: wild brook trout two to ten pounds in catch and release water visited only by thirty-six people a year. Cabins, and showers. Twin otter transportation from Montreal, then a float plane for the farthest reaches. Tundra out the door. Definitely our kind of place.

But what about the cutthroats we knew were waiting in the willow-mazes of the Tongue? Neither of us could get past them. They were luring us back to Wyoming. And what about the fishing at the pass in the northern Wind River Range? We weren't willing to let that go by; what if the road was eventually paved and that precious place lost its character and its wildness before we could get back to hear "our" wolves or see "our" sand hill cranes grazing beneath the glaciers?

It was win-win decision making, and there were many more worthy alternatives that we could have considered, but, in the end, we knew what our summer would be like, and it eased the budding panic I'd felt watching winter slip out of my hands. Michigan: family, friends, farm, and Grayrock, the bamboo rodmakers' gathering on the Au Sable. September at the gathering in Roscoe, new for us. The West sandwiched in between; Ralph Moon, once curator of the Federation of Fly Fishers Museum, was arranging a rodmakers' gathering in Livingston and Tom Helgeson, a friend who deserved a face-to-face thank you for his patient advice, would be fishing the Missouri, two good reasons to visit Montana. And then autumn in New England, beautiful Maine.

Spring wouldn't be so bad, either.

In April, we could go to Nova Scotia or up to scout the Miramichi; we'd done that before. Or, we could take our week off and run to Michigan, check on the family and the farm, and fish the early and usually deserted upper reaches of the Manistee. Coh had gone with us a couple of Aprils ago, and we'd all caught fish, even with Kodiak swimming through the pools. I really don't think most fish worry about dogs, especially if the bottoms are so stable dogfeet can't disturb the sand.

There were lots of April options, but we decided together to stay in Maine. It looked like the ice would be out early, so we could put up the duck boxes and clear trails or canoe along the shore of our pond to look for frogs. Spring peppers burrow in the mud of the bottom to survive the winter, but wood frogs stay on land and freeze solid, protected by natural antifreeze. The pussy willows will have gone by; what about the service berry, blossoming before other shrubs even consider it? David had hope that the F.E. Thomas rod would be ready to dip in varnish by then, at least its first coat, and would like to make a rod for himself for summer (that never happens; someone else always gets his rods).

We talked eagerly of a million plans, but I felt a mild panic begin to rise again. Was winter really almost over?

I was distracted by David pointing out deer tracks over our tracks as we reached a muddy section of the logging road, and then we saw tall white flags bounding off, four big, strong deer. Above them, the sun and its twin, a sundog, at the edge of an incoming front. We picked up the pace. There was wood to bring in before the predicted snow arrived.

In the evening, after replenishing the woodpile, filling the birdfeeders, planing some cane, and finishing the preparations for the week ahead, we settled into rocking chairs in front of the cheerful fire. Kodiak stretched out on his bed between our footstools, soaking up the warmth, pretty much passed out from a great day. We munched on our popcorn and listened to Natalie MacMaster play the fiddle in the background, Cape Breton style. It wouldn't be long and the evenings would be too warm for woodstoves. Nostalgia is a funny thing; sometimes you can feel it coming before the things you love are gone. Seasons, places, friends, family. The only solution is to embrace them thoroughly while it's still possible.

We listened to the weather report before heading to the loft. For Wednesday, the first day of Spring, snow was again in the forecast.

Spring Thaw

*"We could hear the rushing
of meltwater over the dams
before we even stepped into
the morning sunlight."*

W e could hear the rushing of meltwater over the dams
before we even stepped outside into the morning sunlight on the
decks. Kodiak was panting from sunbathing on his dogbed since
six. He barely raised his head when we joined him, our breakfast
in hand. It was forty degrees at seven a.m., and I was wearing my
sunglasses. Spring thaw.

On the first day of the official season, a week before, a front
with a good sense of humor had dumped ten inches of wet snow
on Maine. The thermometer stayed relatively high, however, and
the big banks the snowplow left at the end of our drive never
hardened into snowcrete barriers. We drove the four-wheel drive
truck through them instead of trying to clear heavy wet snow lying
over soft muddy ground, and even the subsequent inch or two,
here and there, couldn't stop the passage of time or the melting
away of winter. The woods were still white, except the wells under
the conifers where the branches had directed the snows outward,
but our clearing was mostly brown again, warm in the morning sun
and outlined nicely with receding snowbanks. Kodiak, drunken
with heat, staggered over to one to cool off.

This was the first morning that the surface of the Big Pond looked gray, soggy. A little sun, a little rain, or a good, strong wind, and the ice would give way. The Last Pond, where the current flows strongest, had been ice free for over a week. A pair of Canada geese had already moved in and was staking claim to the territory. David saw them first, standing quietly on the shelf ice watching me try to negotiate the Hilton, now too wide to jump. A few days later, the gander warned Kodiak to stay on our side of the water. Birds which mate for life tend to look alike, but the gander is usually the taller, more sturdy of the geese. He says 'honk'; she says 'hink'.

The clearing was alive with morning birdsounds. The red-winged blackbirds were in the treetops chirping their 'hey, it's me' calls. They were the first to migrate back and join the chickadees, red breasted nuthatches, gray-eyed juncos, and mourning doves which had over wintered at our feeders. The chickadees' song switched to the two-note, dee-dee, of the spring, and the mourning doves were in the balsams, cooing. Last night, we'd heard a saw-whet owl, Too! Too! Too! Too!, somewhere to the east, and woodcock berzeeping at the edge of the woods. I'd almost stepped on a woodcock on our walk, but it's hard to expect much of a bird whose brain is upside down and backwards. Sometimes, this time of year, we slip out into the darkness when they're strutting about our clearing. We stay very still until the sound of their berzeeps stops and the whir of their spiral flight takes over. Then we run like mad to get to the spot where we anticipate they'll land and wait for them to plop back to earth to see how close we've guessed. They must be reasonably smart because we've never guessed completely right.

I stretched my legs in front of me on the deck and leaned back against the cedar shingles we had nailed on one by one as siding several springs before. They felt warm against my back, and I scooched around to get the most comfortable fit. David sat on the upper deck with his feet near me on the lower one. We were both enjoying a good bowl of Cheerios with a heaping of full spectrum light euphoria; it seemed like ages since we could lounge over Sunday breakfast in sunlight.

The previous Sunday, we'd had our traditional end-of-the-winter breakfast with Barb up the Kennebec in Anson, a small town with a big heart. Each year they celebrate Maine Maple Sunday by calling friends, neighbors, and strangers together for an all-you-can-eat feast of fresh maple syrup, heaps of pancakes, chunks of fried potatoes, two kinds of baked beans, and more. Everyone gathers in the elementary school cafeteria along long tables that would force good conversation if it wasn't already free-flowing. We followed the river on our way back home, passing the monument to Father Rasle near the site of old Norridgewock. The Kennebec was free of ice, and a gravel bar near Old Point was completely covered with geese returning north.

Kodiak joined us on the deck. He tried to stay alert and on guard for the snowshoe hares which might trespass into his clearing any second, but the sun was too much for him, and he flopped over on his side to sleep. He hadn't managed his usual twenty hours of sleep the day before. We'd walked past the fearless woodcock and crossed the roaring Hilton, then west past the old granite barn foundations. Two hundred years ago, would they have been preparing for spring? So many years have passed, it is hard to see the farm for the woods, the road for the trail it has become.

The Hampshire Hill Road had been a veritable quagmire. Kodiak kept to the high banks on either side and tracked a young moose backwards, as is his habit. Our special needs dog. The moose had medium sized tracks and seemed to be in need itself. It wandered here and there, sampling long scrapes of bark from young maples and generally moving aimlessly. Probably last year's calf, fallen from favor and lonely with the approach of spring and its new sibling. Young moose occasionally wander up to our birdfeeders and across our clearing. As luck would have it, Kodiak's approach wasn't entirely in vain. He stumbled on the tracks of a turkey, tracks so large they startled us, and tried to ferret it out until we saw it run across the trail far ahead, and we persuaded Kodiak to turn back toward home.

"Want to cast rods?" David asked. The clearing was free of snow, after all, and the next day would be April first, Opening Day. We wouldn't be fishing, probably not for weeks, but it seemed appropriate to pay homage to the event. Besides, David had been asked to recommend a line for a rod he'd just finished, Jim's 3-piece from the Atlanta airport deal, so we had a legitimate excuse to play.

The rod in question was a seven-foot six-inch three piece built to a Chris Bogart taper he calls the Shenendoah Supreme. David took our cereal bowls into the house and retrieved the rod from his workbench. It was flamed a beautiful mottled brown, and the sunlight raced across the facets. The intent was that it would take a four-weight line, but what about a triangular tapered line? The same? Would it load up better with a five-weight? How about a weight forward line, any difference? And then there's silk. I love the smell of a silk line, like a favorite wool sweater, treated with mucelin to keep it subtle. A bamboo fly rod, a silk line on a 1903-replica Hardy Bougle reel, a sun-warmed, birdsong morning.

I soaked up the sun and watched David string the rod and test a few casts, then offer the rod to me. I was tempted to just watch him cast. The silk line arced back behind him organically, waited, and ran forward again, flowing smoothly, extending to the end. I can't cast like that, though I keep trying. John Long once took my casting style on as a special project at Grayrock, the Michigan rodmakers' gathering, and that helped. Some.

I do catch, and release, fish, but I'm not a picture of the perfect cast. A photographer once made clear my misguided priorities. David and I were exploring a small roadside beaver pond in the Yukon for grayling, fishing off opposite sides of a little peninsula. He has better reflexes and could retrieve the fly between the time the grayling cleared the water and the time it could reach the fly. This ability wasn't necessarily a good thing. On the other hand, I could easily wait until the leaping fish had securely fed and had a fish every time. I was hardly even watching my fly, keeping an eye or two on the alders for big bears, instead. A guy with a medium format Hasselblad and an eye for an angler silhouetted against the setting northern sun positioned his tripod near David and shot until dark. They must have been beautiful photographs, although we never saw them, but I, at least, caught fish.

I accepted the rod from David, thankful that both bamboo and silk are forgiving, and tested the performance. A little stiffer than my Payne 97, maybe less stiff than a Dickerson 7613. A relatively fast, absolutely wonderful rod. I cast to some robins bobbing about the brown grass looking for worms, not flies. Not orange yarn, either. David was readying another reel, so I passed the rod back to him and sat back down near Kodiak's bed. Kodiak, too hot, had abandoned the surface world and slipped under the deck.

We had built the two decks one April just after the snow receded and placed one a stair step higher then the other, two ten by twelve platforms at the front door. Kodiak immediately claimed the world above, perched on the higher one to watch over the clearing. The snowshoe hares claimed the lower world, and he tried to apprehend them there for awhile. Then he must have decided they weren't worth the effort, and he'd lie on his bed above while one or two rabbits lounged in the cool just below. He's not so tolerant of other trespassers. Earlier in the year, he roused us out at midnight, presumably for routine late night relief. I heard David before I smelled the odor from beneath the deck, and we celebrated the first hours of my birthday mixing one box of baking soda with two bottles of hydrogen peroxide and a generous helping of dish-washing soap, lathering Kodiak down, and brushing him off after he'd dried white and skunk free. Skunks should be out and about any day now.

I checked the temperature; it was fifty-five. In spring, that feels like eighty.

David tried a triangular tapered 4/5 weight line next. I use it on my rod sometimes. He didn't seem satisfied, and I thought it was harder to cast. We both tried it again. My rod is easier to load, and it seemed like this gentle line was more suited for it than this rod. Something a little more aggressive, we thought, like a double taper four. It was just our opinion, and, as it turned out, we had no way to test it. We didn't have that line. That's where the rodmakers' gatherings are so handy. Someone has every line and is willing to loan it as well as help test line-weight theories, not that everyone always agrees. Everyone always has fun.

We retired the rod and retreated to the deck, contemplating the work we could be doing on the yard, or, heaven forbid, spring cleaning.

"Scott's in Augusta again today," David said. Scott Chase was exhibiting at the local sportsmen's show, his turn at information and education about cane rods. We'd had a turn at a fly fishing expo the week before. A lot of rodmakers take a turn; it's gratifying sharing bamboo rod construction and lore with new faces, most of whom have a cane rod story to tell. I've never met a bamboo rodmaker who guarded his secrets or turned up his nose at anyone. The idea of a rodmaker even having a secret made me smile. Every night there are scores of e-mails on the rodmakers' list serv, shared information open to any and all. David had just started a new rod based on a F.E. Thomas taper measured by Dennis Higham, advice offered by Tom Smithwick, and adaptations from Wayne Cattanach's Hexrod program. Dennis had even sent photographs.

Come to think of it, we hadn't seen Scott since fall, and we knew he'd have cane rods to cast. Maybe we could just slip down for a couple of hours and tackle the yardwork later.

"Or we could head over to the Penobscot," David said. It seemed like it was almost time for the spring canoe sale.

Epilogue:
The First Days of Summer

More and more, in a place like this,

we feel ourselves a part of wild Nature,

kin to everything.

John Muir

Frogs

"Maine has nine kinds of frogs... May is the best time to find them."

The calendar said it was late May, still part of spring, but for us it was summer. We officially left the Other Season behind on April 10th when we heard spring peepers calling, the first two of hundreds. Now the sun was up late every night, and so were we. The chain of ponds had turned to sparkling waters, and the trails around them were overflowing with a mosaic of green and a collage of returning wildflowers. Wood ducks and black ducks, mallards, teal, and geese, were joined by tree swallows and belted kingfishers, phoebes, bitterns, and whip-poor-wills, Kodiak's evening nemesis. Whip-poor-wills and the moose trotting through the clearing on the way to the pond. We also keep an eye out for snapping turtles laying eggs beneath the birdfeeders. Kodiak brings us painted turtles to release; we don't want him trying it with a snapper.

All during the warm, rainy morning, we dug out maps and looked up internet sites for water levels in Michigan and Wyoming, while working in a few domestic chores. In Maine, winter had completed the cycle, the headwaters falling as snow then melting slowly to nourish our watershed. We had heard rumors of drought elsewhere from the early emissaries to the

West. Then David went back to planing cane, and Kodiak looked out the screen door, pining away. I was with him.

As soon as the sun burned through, Kodes and I headed to the far side of the pond. He led the way at a dogtrot, stopping to sniff the fresh moose tracks on the trail leading out of our clearing. Every needle on the balsam firs was tipped with a drop of rainwater, and the tracks were hoof-shaped pools leading to the pond. We hurried to the Grass Dam, flooded with sun-dancing rapids for the time being. I balanced on the interlaced beaver sticks using a hiking staff thoughtfully placed by the little resident engineers while Kodiak sniffed the far shore for mink or mice.

As we continued up the ridge, I stopped long enough to count the lady-slippers in the glade at the fork in the trail. There were two seed pods left from last year and flowers everywhere, deep pink, exotic and stunning. Forty-two, a remarkable record. Even so, moccasin flowers weren't the objects of our real search today. We were headed to Bull Moose Cove to look for frogs. Our summer researcher, Cathy Bevier, says Maine has nine kinds of frogs. Late May, when the males are vocal, is the best time to find most of them.

The trail along the hemlock covered ridge leads toward the west side of the cove. An American toad had been there hanging out on a sunlit bed of needles off and on all week. He lumbers out of the way whenever we approach, and Kodiak decided to avoid him after the first hesitant sniff. The toad has a parotid gland, which secretes a neural toxin. It makes a bad play toy and a worse meal. Normally, Kodiak likes to investigate small shuffling creatures, but not this one.

Toads breed in the early spring, trilling in a long, high pitch, and hatch tiny black tadpoles in about two days. By the middle of summer, tiny toads take to land. We had been hiking on a low section of the Appalachian Trail a few years ago and found ourselves frozen in the midst of dozens of toads no bigger than a thumbnail, hard to see, easy to squash. Even the hardest of hearts, repulsed by the wart covered adults, would melt over these tiny darlings.

Over the weekend, we'd been up past Rangely Lake, checking out the Kennebago River. We had hiked the area more than we'd fished it and were pretty familiar with the Appalachian Trail past Saddleback Mountain and the Sabbathday Ponds, but the Kennebago was new territory. Ours was the only truck parked at the gate that evening, so we liberated Kodiak from the back and let him poke about while we pulled on our waders. Then we followed the road, easy walking, until we chose an obvious angler's trail to the water. It led to a classic pool, accented with granite boulders and overhung with draping hemlocks. David cast a small caddis at the upstream end; I cast the same fly downstream. Working the pool near one of the boulders, I caught my first landlocked salmon on a bamboo rod. It was four inches long. David paid it the appropriate homage when I called him over as a witness.

It had taken a little more effort than we'd intended.

Wyoming may have its trails through willow thickets, but they're really just a scale model version of the maze of North Woods tote roads the loggers have left in Maine over the last hundred years or more. It was the same deal: we had a good approximation of our target, and we could always spot a mountaintop landmark so we couldn't actually get lost. The little beaver pond we were searching out wasn't much more than a smudge on the page, but we guessed it might be prime brook trout territory. We had a map, although dynamic logging operations had taught us a thing or two about trusting it. In retrospect, we could have just asked someone directions, but, really, what fun would that be?

We had crossed the South Branch of the Dead River on a logging bridge and found the fork in the road indicated on our map, a good sign. We chose the left fork since it was gated against vehicular access, a signal in Maine that foot traffic is welcome, cars are not. We parked and liberated Kodiak from the back of the truck. He was quite pleased.

The sun had just come out just as we dodged around the gate. It had been misty and cold at home. We were both optimistic and hiked past the remote gravel pit, the probable reason for the gate, and on to the next fork in the road. It was hard to tell if our destination pond was nearest the end of the left or right fork since both tote roads appeared to curve and the little smudge was right between them. We reasoned that the hike alone was worth the day's effort, so either would be fine.

An hour later, we had decided to turn back and try the other fork. We'd been in and out of bushwacks down promising but tree-crowded slopes only to find cedar swamps or braided springs, but no pond. At the end of the second hour's return hike, we directed Kodiak to take the other fork and wound our way up a mountain for some incredible views, but no pond. There was Saddleback Mountain, the Bigelow Peaks, Black Nubble, and, to the east just a few miles, the border with Quebec. We had brushed the top layer of snow off one of the few snowdrifts still resisting the change in seasons and scooped up a handful of pure refreshing snowcone snow. Then we had turned back again.

The trip out is always supposed to seem shorter, but Kodiak was hot and dragging by the time he hopped into the back of the truck. We weren't to be beaten, though. We had driven home resolved to return the next day and drive the woods' roads until we found that phantom pond. On that attempt, the ungated fork led us astray only twice, and, after a couple more hours, we had parked the truck, walked down a steep but promising sidetrail, and found the quintessential brook trout pond. There was a major new gravel road leading right to it over on the other side.

Then we had driven over to the Kennebago.

Kodiak and I found Bull Moose Cove occupied by a pair of hunting Great Blue Herons, also admirers of frogs. Kodes was digging under a stump when I crept out on the sphagnum hummocks. I'm not sure what he was after, most likely a scent left by something long departed, but I was in semi-serious pursuit of bullfrogs. We had been hearing their deep, loud, BARRUMPs for about a week, and I wanted to take an informal census: lots this year, less this year, more this year.

Spring peepers started peeping before all of the ice was out along the sheltered side of the cove. They're really hard for me to find, except on rainy nights in car lights crossing the road often with ill-fated raccoons in blind pursuit. Spring peepers are tree frogs, but I've searched for an hour on the streamside brush with no luck, only to find one on the window in the back door when I trudge back from the pond. We canoed one evening, lifted the canoe out of the water, carried it up to the canoe shed, and flipped it on to the rack revealing a peeper clinging to the bottom.

Peepers are about an inch long, tannish with a darker X on their backs. They synchronize their individual little peeps in such a great chorus that they sound like sleigh bells from a distance and are actually irritating up close. They seem to prefer our small alders and wild hazelnut bushes.

Our other tree frog, the Gray Tree Frog, can change in color from green to gray, depending on the background to which it's affixed. Peepers will start their mating calls when the temperature reaches the high thirties; gray tree frogs wait until it's in the sixties. In mid-June, the night will be filled with their trills. On the farm, they live on the screen door up near the porch light. They know where the bugs are at night.

Bullfrogs are comparatively huge, and they're aquatic. They have a noticeable ridge circling behind each ear; the tympanum of the males, only, are bigger than their eyes. This seems odd to me. If the males are trying to call the females, why wouldn't the females have the bigger ears? Maybe the males are more interested in loudly defining a territorial boundary. The juvenile bullfrogs are easy to mix up with the juvenile green frogs, both large, both green, but the ridge on the green frog extends down the side of its back and doesn't outline the ear. Green frogs sound like the twang of a banjo string.

Bullfrogs and green frogs are almost always in the water, whereas the pickerel and leopard frogs are the ones I discover when I'm mowing the grass in our clearing or in our Michigan yard. Pickerels have squarish spots running in two rows running down their backs, and leopards have more randomly placed spots. Pickerels tend to snore when they call; leopard frogs either grunt or sound a rapid tat tat tat tat. I've never seen a leopard frog in Maine.

The mink frog is a burly little frog a bit smaller than a green but much more rare. It occupies a very restricted geographic range. Pretty much understudied, it's thought to inhabit only the northern part of the state and the watershed of our pond. Cathy and her college biology students have been coming out the past two years, arriving just before dark, donning waders and headlamps, and searching for them in the pool at the Grass Dam. The eyes of the minks glow in the lamplight.

Mink frogs look like leopard frogs whose spots have been swirled, brook trout style. They have a strong, musky, minklike odor when handled, and I can hardly get the smell off my hands. They're supposed to be shy, but we've just reached over and picked them up on the Grass Dam without any trouble. Now that I know where they are, I can recognize their hut-hut-hut triplet call. It sounds like two pieces of dry firewood being tapped together. Last night, it was distinct among the brill of the gray tree frog chorus, the gunk of the greens, and the BARRUMP of the bullfrogs.

As I crept along the shore, I found a long sedge with a few seeds dangling from the top. I stripped off all but the three dark terminal seeds, grouped together, and tested it. Almost three feet long, stalk flexible yet strong, nice action, a tempting and realistic looking lure – a frog rod.

The next step was to get into range. The shore was still soggy enough from the afternoon shower that it padded my footfalls if I was careful, but my shadow must have seemed too much like the nearby herons. It sent the frogs quickly to the bottom. I finally saw a waiting bull facing the opposite direction. A grass hummock separated us, and I crouched down to move closer. Kodiak was still absorbed farther up the shore. I carefully fed my makeshift frog rod out through the grasses of the hummock until the dangling seeds were just behind the frog.

This is where I stop to brace myself; I never get used to what follows.

I inched the seeds farther out, holding my breath. Nothing. Then an explosion. I recoiled, startled as always, as the big bull leapt out of the water and grabbed the seeds. It immediately realized the foil and splashed back into the water, but the hubbub had Kodiak pouncing on to the scene. He stood alert, puffed up and woofing, defending his territory from some imperceptible trespasser. Then, perplexed, he looked at me, propped up on my elbows, seated in the warm mud.

"You missed it again," I told him.